WHILE YOU WAIT

While You Wait

A Collection by Santa Barbara Poets

Edited by
Laure-Anne Bosselaar
Poet Laureate of Santa Barbara

Gunpowder Press • Santa Barbara
2021

Published by Gunpowder Press
David Starkey, Editor
PO Box 60035
Santa Barbara, CA 93160-0035

ISBN-13: 978-0-9986458-8-9

www.gunpowderpress.com

Cover Photo and Book Design by Chryss Yost

ABOUT THE SHORELINE VOICES PROJECT: The Shoreline Voices Project publishes Santa Barbara-area poets writing on a specific theme.

Gunpowder Press would like to acknowledge SB Poetry (sbpoetry.net) and generous donors to the SB Poetry fund whose support will provide copies of this book to many of our community's healthcare heroes. We also appreciate the ongoing support of the Santa Barbara County Office of Arts and Culture for poetry in our community, including the Santa Barbara Poet Laureate Program.

Dedicated with gratitude
to our
healthcare heroes

CONTENTS

Foreword by Chryss Yost

I. INVOCATION

Nicolasa I. Sandoval "'Atɨšwɨn, Spirit Helper"   17

II. IT'S OUR NATURE

Sojourner Kincaid Rolle "Zaca"   21
Peg Quinn "What Lies Behind the NO TRESPASSING Sign"   22
Teddy Macker "To the End"   24
Emma Trelles "The Nearest Way"   25
Diana Raab "Pacific Sunset"   26
Jace Turner "Masahide's Moon"   27
Molly Jane Burns "Northern Moon/Moon Set/Morning Moon"   28
Isabelle Walker "Carrizo Plain"   30
Shirley Geok-lin Lim "Prayer For Coyote"   31
Carol Ann Wilburn "First Light"   32
Daniel Thomas "Without Rain"   34
Laure-Anne Bosselaar "Sundowner Wind"   35
George Yatchisin "Even on a Marine Layer Day"   36
Clayton E. Clark "Bloom"   37
Sojourner Kincaid Rolle "In Peace and Gratitude"   38
Susan Read Cronin "Dandelion of Plymouth Rock"   39
Christopher Buckley "Blossoms"   40
Christine Penko "Back Bay, Los Osos"   41
Sojourner Kincaid Rolle "Circle of Painted Stones
        (at La Casa de Maria)"   42
Ellen Chavez Kelley "Elegy for the Groves"   44
Emma Trelles "Novena for Garden Street"   45
Greg Spencer "Like So Many Bananas"   46
Andrea Ellickson "Guardians of the Sill"   47

Gudrun Bortman "Sun Gold, Black Pearl" — 48

Lisl Auf der Heide "The Acorn" — 49

M. L. Brown "Lupini Bean - Extra Large" — 50

M. L. Brown "Christmas Lima Beans" — 51

Rebecca Horrigan "Pumpkin" — 52

Paul Willis "A Very Little Thing" — 53

e. j. "Germination: Apricot Tree" — 54

Maya Shaw Gale "Becoming Tree" — 55

Christina Gessler "What Emerges" — 56

Dairine Pearson "Forest Walk" — 57

Clayton E. Clark "Drought Tolerant" — 58

Gudrun Bortman "A Gnat" — 60

Shirley Geok-lin Lim "California Skies" — 61

Nicolasa I. Sandoval "'Onokoʼ ʼihiʼy: Lizard Man" — 62

Susan Read Cronin "The Inchworm" — 63

Cie Gumucio "Flight" — 64

Paul Willis "A Story of Hands" — 66

Chryss Yost "Senescence" — 67

Christopher Buckley "Sparrows" — 68

Ellen Hayward "The Mourning Dove" — 69

Isabelle Walker "Night Song" — 70

Luci Janssen "Nymphe des Tuileries" — 71

Ronald A. Alexander "Inevitability" — 72

Shelly Rosen "Bathing and Light" — 73

Paul Willis "Golden" — 74

Shelly Rosen "Sousi" — 75

Clayton E. Clark "Genius" — 76

José María Carpizo "Owl" — 77

Enid Osborn "Nighthawk" — 78

Andrea Ellickson "A Crow Named Zorro" — 79

Susan Chiavelli "Dear Deer Hunter" — 80

Ann Bennett "Writing Class at Esalen" — 81

Laure-Anne Bosselaar "Ocean Rooms" — 82

Bruce Willard "History Lesson"   83
Mark Walker "Sailing"   84
Kundai Chikowero "Fresh Breeze"   85

III. From All Angles

David Starkey "Sheltering in Santa Barbara"   89
Laure-Anne Bosselaar "Robert's Keys"   90
George Yatchisin "Micheltorena and San Andres"   91
Christopher Buckley "Driving Up State Street at Night:
    Christmas, Santa Barbara, 1955"   92
Cie Gumucio "Intersections"   94
Christine Penko "Blessings Upon Water"   95
Estella Ye "Playground"   96
Mary Freericks "My Grandson's Visit to Santa Barbara"   98
Perie Longo "Family Soup"   99
Kathee Miller "Searching for My Own Body"   100
Shirley Geok-lin Lim "Social Distancing"   102
Linda L. Holland "Alive"   103
Ibrahim Ibn Salma "Dentist"   104
Pamela Davis "The Waiting Room"   105
Jacqueline Lunianski "Waiting"   106
Ronald A. Alexander "The Kings River"   107
Kathee Miller "Sporty Girl"   108
Ellen Chavez Kelley "Faces"   109
Roy Hildestad "Someday"   110
M. L. Brown "House"   111
Rick Benjamin "Old Pillow"   112
Lois Klein "A Single Chair"   114
Fran Davis "Green Heels"   115
Enid Osborn "Ode to Bob the Shoe Man"   116
Jessica Bortman "Andirons"   118
Margarita Delcheva "Forecast"   120

Peg Quinn "Notes for an Oil Painting:"   121

Bruce Willard "Inverted Root"   122

James Ph. Kotsybar "Open Mic"   123

Jacqueline Lunianski "An Abundance of Tears"   124

Estella Ye "Conversing Under Fresco"   126

Perie Longo "The Blue Poet"   127

Kundai Chikowero "Together for a Future Generation"   128

Linda L. Holland "What is left"   130

Rick Benjamin "if something should happen"   131

David Starkey "The Secret of Longevity"   132

Daniel Thomas "Driving Meditation"   133

Greg Spencer "Silent Retreat in Texas"   134

Estella Ye "A Dream"   135

Bruce Willard "Song"   136

Ann Bennett "Swallowed"   137

Eliot Jacobson "The Book of Snacking"   138

Maya Shaw Gale "Skinny Belt Sings the Blues"   140

Dairine Pearson "Hot Flash"   141

Perie Longo "Old Soul"   142

Louise Borad Gerber "Birthday 70+"   143

Marilee Zdenek "Dancing with Angels"   144

Ann Michener Winter "What I Forgot to Remember"   145

Nancy Lee "Whiteout"   146

Joshua Escobar "Biblioteca"   147

IV. Let Me Count the Ways

Ibrahim Ibn Salma "Cell Speaks"   151

David Starkey "I Imagine my Great-Great Grandfather
     on the Illinois and Michigan Canal"   152

Nancy Lee "Trick or Treat"   153

Carol Ann Wilburn "Doc, My Garden Mentor"   154

Marilee Zdenek "Really?"   156

Claudine Michel "Darkness" 157

Anne Neubauer "From the Backseat" 158

Teddy Macker "Question of the Day" 160

Jace Turner "A Box of Old Photos" 161

Louise Borad Gerber "The Life Force" 162

Mark Walker "Haiku for Bill Lanphar" 164

Ellen Chavez Kelley "Red Horse" 165

Daniel Thomas "Theory of Happiness" 166

Isabelle Walker "If I Wrote A Poem" 167

Sydney Vogel "May Mother Earth Forgive Me" 168

Claudine Michel "Delira" 169

Emma Trelles "Sonnet for Mark" 170

Chryss Yost "Most Importantly, That" 171

George Yatchisin "Pandemic Domestic" 172

Lois Klein "Not-Knowing" 173

Christine Penko "For Doctor Emmerson on the Occasion
of My New Hip" 174

Diana Raab "My Heart Broke Loose with the Wind" 175

Linda L. Holland "Blue" 176

Mark Walker "MV Conception" 177

Fran Davis "Missing You" 178

Margarita Delcheva "Another Recipe for Getting Lost" 179

Diana Raab "His Smile" 180

Susan Chiavelli "Tandem" 181

Anne Neubauer "Twin Souls" 182

Tamara Zdenek Riley "Living in the Fog" 183

Susan Chiavelli "Fallen Fruit" 184

Gudrun Bortman "My Man Buys in Bulk" 185

Eliot Jacobson "Shopping for Godot" 186

Chryss Yost "Furious Bread" 187

Peg Quinn "A Note of Thanks" 188

V. Poems by Children

Delilah Nava "Out Walking One Nice Day"   191
Kaelie Walker "All Yours"   192
Danielle Diehl "Walking on Clouds"   193
Olivia York "On a Beach Side Cliff"   194
Lauren Schweitzer "My Voice"   195
Gracie Meinzer "Gramma, Grandpa"   196
Elizabeth Blakeslee "The Moon Can See Everything"   197
Katherine Casey "River"   198
Barbara Holguin "Slam Poem"   199
Finn Janssen "Rather"   200
Camille Diehl "Clouds Can Be Heaven"   202

V. Poems in Spanish

José María Carpizo "Dios Sol"   205
Eric M. Castro "Efímera"   206
Eric M. Castro "Caballitos de Totora"   207

About the Poets

This collection of poems, written by our community, is dedicated with gratitude to Santa Barbara County's healthcare heroes.

While You Wait originated during what seems now to have been a simpler time. In April 2019, Laure-Anne Bosselaar was selected as Santa Barbara Poet Laureate and she proposed an unusual idea for a collection of poems. "Wouldn't it be wonderful if, instead of having outdated magazines in waiting rooms", she suggested, "we had poems to read while you wait?" David Starkey and I, co-editors of Gunpowder Press, loved the idea. Poems for people as they sat in the waiting room: impatient folks getting routine checkups, patients anxious for their appointments with specialists, or companions worried during their loved ones' examinations. We have all been those people. These poems are meant for you.

Laure-Anne sent out a request for poems, and the community responded. As I read through the manuscript she assembled, I was reminded of everything I love about Santa Barbara. The natural beauty, the architecture and history, and especially the people—all were present in these poems. I imagined how comforting it would be to have these poems to read during an anxious time—like having a friend beside you.

Then COVID-19 happened. Suddenly, it became unsafe to share a book or magazine with others in a waiting room. At the same time, our first responders once again rose to support us, through a pandemic that has lasted month after month. It became even more clear that we were surrounded by heroes: doctors and nurses, of course, but also all varieties of health care workers, were putting their lives at risk.

Laure-Anne had assembled an excellent collection of poems, which we wanted to share with the community. We figured out that we could create an "no touch" online version of the anthology that people would be able to read safely while they were in waiting rooms through their phones. We also decided to print copies of the collection as gifts for some of the many people working to keep us safe. Thanks to the generosity of the Santa Barbara community, we will be able to donate more than 1,000 print copies of the book for free to health care workers. The poems are also available free online to read at *whileyouwait.org*.

Of course, our health care heroes have been here all along, protecting us. One winter evening in 2018, I was watching the starlit sky for a planned launch from Vandenberg AFB. Suddenly, I felt a weird, crampy pain in my chest. I paced for almost an hour, foolishly hoping to "walk it off." Finally, my husband drove me to the Emergency Room at Cottage Hospital. While I was having a diagnostic angiogram, I'm told I went into cardiac arrest. Dr. Michael Shenoda recognized that I was experiencing a heart attack due to an extremely rare condition called Spontaneous Coronary Artery Dissection (SCAD). Surgeon Peter Baay performed an emergency triple bypass. My good fortune in being part of the 10% of people to survive SCAD is due in no small part to having excellent medical support when I needed it. I dedicate my part in this project to honor Dr. Shenoda and Dr. Baay and their teams, as well as to my family, who spent many anxious hours in the waiting room, unsure if I would recover.

We are blessed in Santa Barbara to have excellent medical facilities including Sansum, Cottage Hospital, Santa Barbara Neighborhood Clinics, and others. We also recognize that the pandemic demands a broad definition of "first responders." It is not just the emergency room doctors, but an entire system that supports us: nurses, orderlies, administrators, janitorial crews, dispatch, and many, many others. Many of our friends and neighbors have stepped up to provide daycare, help with grocery shopping or other errands, working extra hours. Others have seen their paychecks dry up as tourism and restaurants are shut down. The challenges are massive and ongoing.

As poets, we recognize the power of language. We hope these poems will help you through the challenges you face while you wait, whatever and whoever you are waiting for.

Chryss Yost
Co-editor, Gunpowder Press

I.

INVOCATION:
SAMALA CHUMASH POEM

ʻAtɨšwɨn, Spirit Helper

ʻAtɨšwɨn, spirit helper,	ʻatɨšwɨn
sing me to life.	šutiwɨy atɨkiy
I am new again,	ʻikɨmin apiwil
born to your embrace.	qot'in tiwolk'om
Bare, no shame.	šeqeč sunaxnisin ʻinsil
Gifts you carry softly,	nukuti maqsuwayan
thundering from electric skies.	siwon ʻalapay
Bolts of lightning flashing.	štɨx a soxk'on
Storms rush the raging tides.	išʰɨlɨn suxina'n
Built me a sacred home,	ʻaphʰan šawi'l
crystal in sapphire seas.	xɨlɨ'w yolin sxa'min
Pearls surface, glistening	ʻatɨšwɨn napay ʻiqšt'a'n
emerald green.	ʻaqulapšan
ʻAtɨšwɨn, spirit helper,	ʻatɨšwɨn
sing me to life.	šutiwɨy atɨkiy
Revelation, you are.	ʻalulkuw,
Guardian of ruby fire,	qilik yutakla'
Keeper of ancient stars.	nukuti moloq ʻaqiwo
ʻAtɨšwɨn, spirit helper,	ʻatɨšwɨn
sing me to life.	šutiwɨy atɨkiy

II.

It's Our Nature

Poems about Plants, Animals, the Skies & Seasons

Zaca

...Therefore the way of the soul...leads to the water,
to the dark mirror that lies at the bottom."
—Carl Jung

The mountain obsidian shale
cups the green water
in the palm of its oddly shaped hand

Mountain immovable ageless
harboring sage and chapparal trails
where Chumash elders roam

Mountain with sphinx gaze
watching a million tides recede
watching the endless trek and settle

The Seraphim whisper
Echoes dance among the willows
looping the angelic harmony

The lake ancient as the runted hills
gathers the oldest secrets of the valley
close to its cleavage

Open to any soul questing
touching bottom a costly discovery
deep in the quiet place

What Lies Behind the NO TRESPASSING Sign

My intent was respect
for the red-edged sign
wedged in the bush,
TURN BACK.

But there was open sky
with new brightness,
and a tan, dusty path curving
with a certain allure
that's hard to resist.
So I entered.

Cattails swamped the creek
standing tall, at attention,
under inspection
of blue-winged dragonflies.

In a glance a Great White Egret
was sailing about twenty feet
above the path—straight toward me.
Swaying, as if it, too, were caught
in the single note of the trail's
rhythmic movement.

I stopped.
Hoping to blend with the scenery.

Its broad wings pumped,
rowing closer.

As it moved by,
the light in its eye
blinked once,
a wink of approval,
a nod in passing.

To the End

i say praise
praise the sound of this rain
i say lament
grieve shake collapse
throw up your hands
but praise
praise this hard passing rain
the prosperous near sounds
of dripping-from-eaves
the surround sound
of clement iris roar
and let the wonder come
that still it falls upon us
down to this earth
night's kindness
total mother
filling the creek for the badger
gracing the sleep of your daughter
running its hooves on the tin roof
of the barn
hear it leave now move out
towards the islands
drifting shawl of mercy
drawn over anchored boats
bird-spattered buoys
touching the back of a dolphin as it rises
for a breath
touching the slick maximal back
two drops on the dorsal
which now slips back
under
into the cold
faultless
cathedral

The Nearest Way

Would I consume what I really wanted
only nothing would be left. I am many pigments
maybe you should figure them out, I'm spent from shining
except when I depart, then my antelope heart sends me
north to the high lands, where I glow unseen among the pines.

Pacific Sunset

Tonight I sit on the beach
    at the cusp
        of yet another sunset.

How many does it make now,
    as I approach my septuagenarian years?
        I ask the horizon with its flat edges.
            In its stillness, it stares back at me,
          devoid of answers.

            Nature is that way—
              it gives us the needed
                sanctuary but guards answers
                  as I watch my reflection
                  in its stillness.

Masahide's Moon

The great Japanese poet Masahide wrote:

"Now that my house has burned down
I can see the full moon."

Well, that's a loose translation & my mantra
these days of darkness & loss & quiet isolation.

One must seek out the bright spots
like the buzz of blazing mustard fields in bloom,

or pocket of sky brushstroke blue & fading
over the bundled couple slowly walking hand

in precious hand, like the lyrical duet
in the second movement of Schumann's Cello Concerto.

How twilight gives way to evening's riot of stars
pushing through the black dread of nothingness

& rising there Masahide's Moon.

Northern Moon

Having dreamt
of turning
into rain

and surrounding
myself with
my potent body

I began sipping
the world
from my own
two hands.

* * *

Moon Set

Crescent moon
curving your
orange spine
toward ocean
so close to earth
that I
don't know
how much more
time we
have together
before you set
your full back
splashing
into the blue
midnight water.

* * *

Morning Moon

looking out
from beneath
the sky
you have held
your place
all night

while I rested

never leaving
your sight.

Carrizo Plain

I wonder why I like lonely places
like grasslands, so empty you can almost hear
ten miles beneath your feet the earth's plates
grinding and pushing the dusty Temblors clear
to Mexico. A quarter-million acres
of native grasses withering at your feet.
Wind whistle whirls granules of dirt
in little twisters like ghosts of Chumash
dances. You have to shut your eyes tight.
When the blunt-nosed lizard scrams for the nearest
rat hole, it reminds me how my sisters ditched
and teased till I went running to my room
thinking one of them would check on me
and waited while the moon set through the trees.

Prayer For Coyote

Snatching fast fleeing bunnies,
Digging at shallow mole-holes,
Licking the dew-brushed bayberry
Branches when the creek bed molts
Into shattered baked clay ruts:
Mistress of opportunity,
Her whelps' unceasing whimper cuts
Her, and she must dare where she
Cannot go—under the fence through
Damp colored ground. Ancestress,
Teach her to live when her dugs, milk-less,
Hang low; to pad, jaws and sinews
Strung, an old cat, caught in the daisies,
Across the creek, back to her babies.

First Light

In the night—crashes,
harsh streaks of light.
So violent a thrashing
that time cannot
be measured.
Even clocks stop.
Trees hang heavy,
drip vestiges of wetness,
no footprint
on lamp-lit pavement.

The last darkness gives way
to a pale and cool first light,
the greens and blues,
reds and yellows
all about to awaken.

The air washed clean,
birds try out their voices
from the tops
of their tree perches.
An unsteady chorus
gathers itself up
as each flock
rises to praise.

The brilliance!
That oh so brief
and delicate spark

of time when
darkness turns to light
and silence to sound
that wrestles in
another day.

Without Rain

After two hundred days without rain,
the patter on the roof is a beatific
drum, calling the thirsty to leave
their worldly trappings. I step out
of my shell of beams and boards, and revel
with the swaying palm trees, dust
washed away from our brittle fronds.
Slowly, the flagstone steps open
pools of sky, many mirrors,
in which we truly see our foibles,
our faults, our brave love.

Sundowner Wind

Three days now & the sundowner stubborn: a hot hiss
in the jacaranda. It's in bloom. There is no blue
            like this one, dusted by drought & dusk
                        but flowering all it can—

raising its fists to the other blue—up there—sun-fraught,
            contrailed, hazed & exhausted with light,
                        but there, unfailingly there.

        The streets are empty, but for a mockingbird on a roof, he too
                        doing all he can, singing to the scorched mountains
pockmarked by the Tea Fire.

The sundowner danced
            with that fire for days,
        its flames still a rage in my old friend's eyes:
            she lost all she had to it.

I think of her often, bent over, sifting
            pottery shards from her house's ashes & finding
                        solace there. My god: solace—in so little.

The sun's down. The wind dies in the tree.
            I thumb the two wedding bands on my finger, have them
                        do their little dance together: tiny rings
            in a stillness that can't silence everything.

Even on a Marine Layer Day

One of our nasturtium
out its heart bleeds
an even brighter orange
you have to get close to
to be sure it's not shadow,
some glory you just hope
to glimpse, inadvertently
revising the world. So
when you realize it's real,
gorgeous and mindless
and without a need for you,
you remember it's just
a showoff weed, a re-seeder
with the good sense
to be indiscriminate.

Bloom

Out there in the dark
beside the garden path
Night-Jasmine blooms.

Do you see their sparkle?
See the soft kisses
they lay on each other
lit beneath the moon?

They relax some when no one
looks, when no one admires
or praises them.

Profound, almost
invisible, little Goddesses
ready to soften the blow
if you stumble. They'll lift
and cradle you, show you
the stars, perfume
your end of day
ruminations.

But don't get too
attached, stay too long,
try to hold on forever. Their
sweet scent has been known
to cause sentimentality, nausea,
even send headaches downwind.

In Peace and Gratitude

(Near Painted Cave)

In a perfect world,
trees grow straight up—
limbs lifted in perennial worship.

At Pulpit Rock,
beneath a solitary pew,
a tarantula resides

praising the round world.
A lizard, lone like me,
sunning on a solitary boulder.

Purple profusions grow wild here—
spawned by an invisible philanthropist.
grafted onto rocky terrain

Not without sound
avians flitter in solitude
above our proud wandering.

Centuries of ancestral footsteps
foretell our own destiny.

Lo' the sleek manzanita
apothecary to the realm—
keeper of the species.

Caretakers and dandelions in residence
among the trees and rocky nooks,
'long the meandering Marie Ignacio Creek.

Dandelion of Plymouth Rock

We came over together
on the Mayflower

the dandelion and I.

Kindred spirits,
both blonde,

now blanching,
full-sphere white crowns—

that ride the wind
instead of the waves,

our hair-like parachutes
in search of a moss-covered rock
on which to land.

Blossoms

Today, Sunday, I am all right.
Walking the cliffs by the old estates,
I think the lime trees seem less worried
with winter, its basket of less and less.
Grapevines climb a whitewashed pergola
forgetting the month's cold.
And after all the afternoons
shut in with work, it doesn't matter
that I have these tattered sleeves
or that the dust along the orchard paths
dances up to me like an old friend.
Because the sand-colored birds
are ramshackle at the feather
and still get away
to the salt and pepper rocks at the point.
Because the mussels which divide out
have a heart untied from their bones.
Because riches fall
even to the least of us.

Back Bay, Los Osos

Marsh & mudflats   pickle weed
& eel grass   wet feathers
pressed into sand

Violet jellyfish the size
of a dinner dish
White egrets   mallards   terns

Mexican polkas leak
from a radio a workman
forgot in the field

Flat bottomed skiffs
greet morning's tide
wait for her water to yield

& there on the shore
two Monterey Pines
lean as if falling together.

Circle of Painted Stones (at La Casa de Maria)

Standing in this circle,
we clasp hands.
A momentary silence.
Then in hushed reverence,
> we honor each stone;
> we utter each name;
> we hallow each memory.
We salute our common grief.

Gentle clover—beauty's emissary—
encircles each remembrance.

Here among the memory stones,

> we consider the years
> they might have lived;

> consider the hands
> that might have worked
> toward healing;

> consider the feet
> that might have strode
> out of the dark tunnels
> into the light.

Here familiars congregate in
disparate spaces.

On my writing hand,
as if to guide it, a fly lands.

A crow babbles in unison
with the sweet whistle of
a wren. A duet of opposites.

Here we speak a common tongue;
the language of sorrow and loss
and, too, hope.

Elegy for the Groves

We woke each morning to the blossomed air,
the grove across the street our favorite lair.
We ran and hid, got lost and did not care.

The fallen fruit was breakfast for the crows,
the trees were fat and planted in long rows
of fertile dirt that stuck between our toes.

We knew the smell of smudge pots in the cold
since frozen air would kill them, we were told,
so California burned to save her gold.

They came and cut the groves out in a wave
of tract home fever, didn't even save
our grove. The trees are dead. It's all been paved.

The pictures on the crates depict this scene:
snowcapped mountains, clean air, sparkling streams
and groves that only grow inside a dream.

Novena for Garden Street

Barely dressed in the creamy mantilla of ornamental pear
Trees, and cold rain, and agaves unfurling their tongues
To the sun, spring inches up Garden Street, a hesitant bride
Pure in her faith that better days await, they do, and we will
All emulate the hummingbird's rapture for hibiscus, agapanthus,
The coral bell vines that stitch every chain link into a new tapestry.
Crickets will gather in their unseen choirs, the clock will keep
Its forward march, and from a small apartment near the park
A fellow human will play guitar and sing something about
The long train ride home, something about arrival.

Like So Many Bananas

The
summer
peels away
like so
many
bananas.
A pratfall
here. A
smoothie
there. Days
ripen so
fast our only
choice is to
freeze them
or throw them
in the compost.
Such waste,
unless we eat,
eat, munching
down the fruit
of the day
at its peak
of tangy
good-
ness.

Guardians of the Sill

She loved how the Latin names felt on her tongue
enchanting and languorous, like:

Ferocactus cylindraceus
    Fire
        Barrel
            Cactus

Other times it was their common names that made her laugh
pure sweetness
like talking with caramel stuck
between her teeth:

    Hen and Chicks
        Sempervivum
    Irish Mittens
        Opuntia monacantha

Lying in her bed
prickly silhouettes along her windowsill
soft chenille blanket tucked up to her chin
she watched over them
and they over her.

Sun Gold, Black Pearl

       August tomatoes fill my blue pottery bowl—
Cherokee purple   Black Krim
                         & that Brandywine!
      Orange and crimson   brushed like a sunset—
a madness of color.

Sun-sated   there's the ghost of pungent vine.

I slice into a heart-shaped fruit   halved
                  the flesh glistens   blood shades
seeds like zygotes
             tight in their cradling chambers
                            luscious ripeness

And O! that sweetness   moist   heart of summer

The Acorn

Awesome the power of the acorn
dropped from great heights
into earth too dry to nourish.

Minuscule the rootlets
it sends out
when the first rains
seep between dead leaves.

How does it know
to push sharp shoots
through layers of soil

to consort with the sun
as buds unfold into green
to weather winds
and searing summers?

Can it count the circles
forming beneath
expanding bark

the branches
that shelter roots
deep and secure?

Stronger than time
the trunk of the oak
sprung from an acorn
small as a pearl.

Lupini Bean - Extra Large

Lupinus mutabilis

You leave us to float in salted water for days.
Pale, misshapen rounds, legume belugas
in your glass mixing bowl. We watch

as you head to work in the morning,
gym bag, briefcase, umbrella, then charge
through the door at night, drop everything

to the floor. It's been raining for weeks, you're soaked.
You do not notice how beautiful we are when wet.

Christmas Lima Beans

Phaseolus lunatus

Their shape a wave, a curl of sea. Their skin
    a splash of brown and feathered sweep

on white sand beach, alive, alive—O!
    Oval gems rocking in my palm.

I close my hand around them, long for you
    to touch them, too, tell me what wondrous thing

they call to mind, hear the intake of your breath
    at beauty I can barely describe.

Some also call them Temple of Peace;
    I find no proof of this. They disturb

with desire—to touch, to press to lips,
    to worry them to moth wings that I might see

their magic, wind-spread, like your ashes
    above a swerve of water.

Pumpkin

It's sunny, but I bought a pumpkin.
Through the busy, hot, impersonal parking lot
where no fall leaf makes its mark
I cradle the buoyant, bright
unmistakably orange gourd.
Into my dusty car,
it seems to smile in the shotgun seat.
Street parking only today.
One hand fastened tightly to the just-might-break grocery bag
the other lightly hugging my carrot-colored companion close to my chest.
It seems to balance on my arm
as we begin our limp-walk home.
Cars respect the pumpkin.
Like a yellow light, they cautiously pump the brakes in its tangerine glow.
Heading up the concrete stairs, one side of me drags
the groceries, the crumpled to-do list, the leaking water bottle.
The other side of me floats
like an orange buoy, the round accessory lifts us up
above the stained, green Astroturf
to the top of the stairs
where the blue sky and magnanimous mountains stand in loyal greeting.
Where the gentle palm trees wave us in, swaying in the breeze
that might just have a hint of a chill.
Perched on the coffee table, the pumpkin sits.
Making no demands.
Accomplishing nothing.
Offering everything in its silent, simple cheer.

A Very Little Thing

A very little thing is rolling
down the street at dawn,
some little yellow thing, a lemon,
rolling down the center
of the street from the little
grove just up the hill.

Has the cold of the morning
snapped its hold upon the tree?
Or did someone toss it, carelessly,
to see it mind its little business,
bundling down the little street?

Will it fall in the little creek
at the bottom and ride
the current to the sea?
Will it float there—a lemon buoy,
a yellow bobber, a little
sour island on the salt rim
of the little world?

Germination: Apricot Tree

Dark, damp, alive with decay underground
Body asleep with curious lined skin
Subconsciously growing with unheard sound
She fell here softly, from her giant kin

She sits here untouched, protected
Her curves, her edges all warped and dry
She waits for rain to find her dissected
Mothers all surrounding, strong and so high

May her buds be so large, and so robust
Her many green wings of waxy faces
She dances from her womb, up to greet us
We guide her up to seek the best places

Pulsating and torn was her veined shell
When it left her, she knew she'd worn it well.

Becoming Tree

(Inspired by a line from Sharon Olds' poem "Pine Tree Ode")

As if a tree were a spurt from the earth, a heart's gush,
a prayer arrow petitioning the sun for its blessing,
a testament to the power of standing one's ground,
I press my cheek against the papery skin
of the ancient sycamore down by the creek,
as if it could fill me with strength,
give a direct transmission of having made peace with time,
as if it could teach me how to be still in the midst of life's storms,
as if my own legs could pull nourishment from the dirt and the stones
and I could become silent accepting witness
to the river of years flowing by.
I spread my arms in a wide embrace of the sycamore's body,
as if I could pull her into my heart,
fuse her straight spine with my own, grown crooked
with the twists and turns of an irregular life,
as if I could remember myself back into the forest of my past
where I could converse with her kin, know the language of birds,
become a refuge for the wandering and the wild,
as if I were a spurt from the earth with no thought for my self
and inseparably merged with the world.

What Emerges

In the quiet
I breathe, breathe,
my feet on the cushion below me,
the carpet below that
atop the flooring of this building
resting
above
dirt
and tree roots
that dig down into the center of the earth.

Those roots hold it all together?
So the dirt stays,
so the building resting upon the
dirt
bound by the roots
stays still,
holding this room
with its carpet
cushion
my feet
and legs
and the rest of me?

When all is gone
and all that's left
is the breath that breathes me, whispering:
You are here

another breath
emerges
to take the place
of the one
before.

Forest Walk

At the end of the day, the forest calls me home. I enter the trail obediently, moving fast and alone, not seeing the unfolding masses falling away at the edges of my vision. I begin, every bright leaf moving towards me, the rocks rising up to meet my palms. In twenty breaths I am loosed, body shifting left and right, west and east, always in forward motion. Thoughts spill out and over my head. There is music in my ears, all sounds tuned to each tree, to bark and trunk, to each curving green branch, to the shale and water, to the soft edges and beyond those edges, and then resounding to the sky above. Everything is green and a thousand colors of green. Even the browns and grays and whites are green. Each leaf is a breath, all the woods a great crowd gathered around me, drifting away out of sight. The rocks are covered with transparent skin, pressure sensitive and warm, with roots snaking through the places where they touch the earth. The poison oak is quiet and evil. The stones of the stream wait patiently, offering their backs to open palms. The water keeps its distance, knowing its cold crystalline beauty. I am shoulders, legs and lungs, brain unraveling, eyes ever more dazzled. The ground springs instantly back under each step, every footfall a micro-negotiation of weight and balance, achieved in an instant and then forgotten. Heart and mind switch places, rising and falling in alignment with the trees. I might be warm or cold. Someone nearby is thirsty and panting. Thoughts become feelings, become thoughts again and diffuse into the air. I feel that thing called awe, and I feel ordinary and out of breath. All around is endless green unfolding that refuses to stop, settle and limit itself, a living being beyond impression, beyond words, beyond me, beyond capture and negotiation, only release.

Drought Tolerant

A Canary Island Pine, stands
in my back yard, tall as God, long feet,
deep rooted in the dry soil, drenched
only by sun.

My neighbor called the tree a nuisance,
an immigrant, was glad she didn't have one. Love
is subjective, I guess, a formless shape-shifter
always on the move. I admit it, I love her,
my immigrant tree.

I see the tree as a her and sometimes
as a him. Let's call her from here on out
Pine. Together, Pine watches, looks down
on the frenetic scurry of people and animals
below, accepts everything nature throws
Pine's way.

Slowly Pine produces cones, fruit
according to the squirrels
who devour them.

Birds sing on Pine's branches, make homes
in Pine's ample arms. Stolid body, curved
at the hip, lower limbs droop and wave
with the weather, with every rhythm
of every day.

Summer is on the way to warm Pine who
welcomes every season, grows without

lessons, without lectures or Canary Island Pine
school, on Pine's own terms, in Pine's own
good time.

Pine is a tree of knowledge,
an autodidact, born knowing,
the same as my young, wild son.

A Gnat

Curled in my leather chair I relish
a poem about wilderness,
while a midget of a fly nags my face,
nearly inhaled on the tide of my breath.

Incessant wheeze around my head—
I purse my lips, huff it away, sniffle
to rocket it off.   Still it persists,
now lights on the page—

I slam the book shut.
And there it is now—
right between *huckleberries* and *bears*.
Flattened. A spread-winged black dot
like a tiny crucifix   pointed at me.

California Skies

(The Holiday Fire, Goleta—July 7, 2018)

skies

    with no clouds

skies

    bleached by sun

skies

    heavy with winds

skies

    black in the hills

skies

    red in the blue

skies

    hissing in brush

skies

    crackling in branch

skies

    noisy with wings

skies

    dry with white rain

skies

    roofless, rueful—

        only

            sky.

'Onokok' 'ïhï'y: Lizard Man

'Onokok' 'ïhï'y, lizard man, how clever you are.
First, a silent witness, watching us.
New friends, dreaming in vivid color about tomorrow. Hearing the music
      of fresh voices singing.
Perched with the birds on the budding vines above us, you bide your time.
Choosing just the right moment to make your appearance.

'Onokok' 'ïhïy, lizard man, how bold you are.
You drop from the sky, and on to our table.
Messenger of a memory I buried – the story of why we have your hands.
Sky Coyote and Eagle wanted us to have theirs. The moment no one saw
      you coming, you
slipped in, imprinting your hand onto the rock that was the mold for ours.
Today, you bless us again. Beacon from another world, beaming the light
      of our ancestors.

The Inchworm

Hanging by a thread
        that's how I find you.

You light upon my shoulder.
        I will carry you farther

than you've ever been before.
        I will take you up a trail

lined with bougainvillea.
        Your eyes will not see

the beauty spread before us—
        they will only sense
light and dark. You will turn into a moth.

Attracted by the light, in the dark
        you will fly into a flame

and bring with you no memory
of what you are now:

a small green stripe, stretching out
        to become a full inch

in the immeasurable world
        that lies—vast
                beyond my shoulder.

Flight

afternoon crochets light across
the distance it spans

tangled in sticky strands
          is an autumn leaf snared
in faerie filament flung across the driveway?

no, not a piece of autumn
but a yellow-gold monarch caught
midflight

how many hours has it been
tethered ? trapped?

Intent to free the winged beauty
glasses askew, I become Valkyrie
armed with rake and broom

aiming high and wide to break the silk netting, save
the quaking creature in fight for life—
but, then suddenly still

the world is cruel, laments the new quiet
I spot trickster-spider in a corner of his murderous snare
and decide to rob it of its prey

one defiant swipe
the silk-strong tendrils tear
so, there

and to my astonishment—enlivened wings
rise and flutter off   no worse for wear

angels cartwheel
the spider scowls
          I scowl back
 and shake my rake
like a backyard Brunhild might

A Story of Hands

Our hands, say the Chumash,
were supposed to be coyote paws.

Coyote had won the argument
of who would provide that part of us.

At the last second, lizard,
who had been very quiet,

reached out to touch the white
stone of our creation in the sky

and left his print. That's why
our hands are lizard hands.

That's why lizard keeps diving
down into cracks in the rock.

Coyote is still wanting
to get his paws on him.

Senescence

Like most of our kind, we stay in now:
The old, the higher risk, the fatalists.

The moon slivers down and fills again with light.
Our car is slowly buried in a litter of leaves.
The garden lush with our attention.

There are birds we know by name: Hummingbirds
and scrub jays and still one tattered hen
who surprised us both by outliving her flock.

Tonight's guest trots along the fence: a possum
umbered by the sunset heads toward the plums.

Already she is staking out her claim.

Sparrows

Like the poor, they are with us always ...
what they lack in beauty is theirs
in good cheer—tails like pump handles
lifting them first among songsters, chiding
city light or roadside to evening's praise.
Gristmills, hardy gleaners, but for them
the weeds and thorns would find us wanting.
Ragmen to the wind, Sophists of the twig,
they pause to bathe in the ample dust,
and accept the insect as relish to the seed.
So it is becoming to not be too fastidious
when you are rapidly inheriting the earth.

The Mourning Dove

Early dawn   I walked alone
barefoot on warm pavement
shorts on my summer legs
and came upon a mourning dove

I'd heard one from afar
many times before   its crooning
a soft blanket on my shoulders

I followed   careful   silent
Violet feathers shone pink and gold
under grey sky and faded moon

Then   it fluttered and sang for me
full-throated and pure
an offering   a psalm of sadness
and light

Night Song

A mockingbird sang
in the night last night—
one song after another
never pausing.
In bed I was blinking
into words I wanted
to take back,
the broken Puiforcat.
Exhaling, vapors filled the room
till the spirit of my father's second wife
(the one who stomped
the amaryllis seedlings)
appeared in tennis whites,
smug and grinning
in the corner.
But I couldn't comprehend the bird
crooning into nothing,
not another bird sound around
or hint of breeze or dawn,
just breath and ears
and string of borrowed songs.

Nymphe des Tuileries

Camille Saint-Saëns hums softly,
he strolls sun-dappled alleys.
He searches for a theme as notes promenade
across his mind and block his pathway.
—notes ajumble until composed—
Playful sounds of a nearby fountain
entice him forward to the water's edge.
He pauses with fermata-arched brow,
glories at a white-brocaded ripple,
tilts his head nearer the water,
sees a glint of iridescence and smiles.
She flaunts her gossamer tail,
lures him closer with her beauty—
splashes his face with a mirthful flick!

She fancies to catch herself a suitor,
blows flirty, bubble kisses to make him swoon,
peeks coyly through the liquid veil,
moves with the grace of Anna Pavlova,
tantalizes him with swirling pirouettes,
bursts into a grand jeté aquatique!

"Bravo!" He claps with effervescent delight—
her lyrical movements beguile him,
flood his every heart chamber with music.
"Enchanté, ma petite chérie tu es ma muse."

Inevitability

There are days when fighting
is pointless.

Despite the odds
despite all the obstacles you conjure
despite all your self-imagined frailties
and all the bamboozlement
you throw in the way

the world will not be muted
or restrained or even
reasonable.

No matter how fiercely you struggle
to deny the fact
the world will make evident that you
are loved.

As you traverse the pier, flounders
rise to the surface, offer you those sucking wet Hollywood kisses
fishes make to the air.

In the gracious wood porcupines
lay down their quills and bears
bless you in Esperanto.

In the painted desert chuckwallas
crawl out of their granite
towers to greet you, saguaros whisper
your name and rattlers

sing to you Puccini.
They will not be denied.

You will know.

Bathing and Light

Her croak resonates
above the crashing water
as the green iridescent frog
takes a shower
beneath the cascade

In her imagination
she is bathing beneath
Victoria Falls
before meeting her lover
for a night on the town

On filtered light she
slips and slides through the leaves
then, colliding with rushing water,
sparkles in rainbow radiance,
rolls and falls with each drop
    —drop after drop—
and races downstream riding
on shimmering bubbles
into her paramour's embrace.

Golden

My red-furred dog is floating, paddling
under the dark branches of bay, the summer alder.

How green the pool he courses in, circling
in the eddies of leaves, bits of foam

from a careful rapid catching the corners
of his mouth. My red-furred dog, he

smiles as he always does in the pool of green,
this quiet pool that is lucent as an apple kiss.

Sousi

Already in a frazzle over lost luggage
I notice my connection flight
is canceled jeopardizing my
morning business meeting in New York
I swell like a rocket primed, burst into flame.

Then I see her
and realize she is just what
a tense traveler needs
She squeals and wiggles,
almost giggles, as she approaches.
To accompany her red-painted toenails,
she wears a pilot style uniform
or a dancer's tutu.
She changes to yellow toenails
when sporting her yellow polka-dot bikini.
Today, though, her wardrobe
reflects purple people eater Thursday
including a purple sari,
purple under garments
and purple nails to match

Sousi, a therapy pig, is part of the Wag Brigade,
animals who roam airport terminals
wearing vests saying "Pet me."
After strokes of her pink smooth skin,
my blood pressure plummets to a pleasing level.
I manage to secure a new flight several hours later
than my original, meaning I will miss
a good night's sleep. Still I am in good spirits,
my time with Sousi well worth all the worry.

Genius

This old dog lies
on the couch next to
the Tao Te Ching
and does

—nothing—

as though
she's already
read it and taken
it in.

Owl

There's no distance between darkness and silence

The violence of the sea floods my ears
There's nothing to grapple with.

If it transformed into words
what would the owl advise
in her sleepless wisdom?

Her eyes interpret in dark
the guileless vibration that suspects
the intoxicating void of what is not said
Her silent glide reaches us.

Nighthawk

Driving into Roswell, New Mexico
June 2, 2002 10:30 p.m.

At the end of a thousand miles,
I skim the mesa in my night-colored car
  with the windows rolled down.

That mist of pretty stars in the distance
  is my hometown.

Though this is not the place to offer me
  any kind of a welcome,
I go for that little galaxy,
  roughly in the shape I remember it,
  making a heart in the big river basin
  where water and oil lie secret under the earth.

And off to the north, lightning
  flashes in the bellies of low-lying clouds.
That slow strobe of golden light
  fills me with resolute joy.

Fields run alongside the road, opening wide,
  and the smell of alfalfa on a humid summer night
  changes my mind about a lot of things.

What things? Can't tell you now...

but I swear by this sweet road,
  I am the child who ate this dirt.
  I am the dear daughter who was hankered for.
  I am the prodigal, singing my Southern hymn.
  I am the nighthawk, winging my way home.

A Crow Named Zorro

The crow sneaks a french fry from the garbage bin
and dances on our rooftop—
that rascal
scrit-scratches on the tile
black feathers fanning out like a cape.

That dashing rogue,
a Zorro in his black mask
fooled us again
found the french fries
even though we hid them
deep inside the bag.

Then, our hungry hero
swoops down
for another bite
as if
we don't know
who he really is.

Dear Deer Hunter

My granddaughter wishes to capture a speckled fawn like Bambi
and make it her pet. When I was her age I loved Bambi, too.
The movie still plays in the womb of my shadow.

I'm five again, sobbing in the Crest Theater, Mother pulling me
up the aisle through darkness, the forest fire blazing behind us—
Bambi's mother dead on the ground.

A herd of deer roam these hills. We watch their liquid eyes watching
us, the keepers of the roses. Sometimes they step closer,
as if they might abandon their wildness and eat from our hands.

Caitlyn practices throwing a lasso over the fence post by the barn.
When she wears her cowgirl boots and hat she sees with the eyes
of a hunter. Today she loops her lasso in a circle on the lawn,

fills it with the deers' favorite roses—the pale yellow Poet's Wife,
no ordinary floribundas. She waits on the other end of the rope,
determined and ready to pull it—waits in the want and wishing

on the edge of our canyon—in a place where every rustle is
something about to happen, something ready to step into her
sweet trap. Her shadow touches my shadow—

black silhouettes painted on green lawn. Bambi cavorts
in the background, the music playful, the place in the movie
long before the forest fire and the hunter's gun.

Writing Class at Esalen

To the south on the ridge of the hill is a wash
 of sun and below the dark ocean murmurs and groans.

There is hope here with friends
inside, away from the rain, a reprieve;
but I'm pulled outside,
focus on a grebe in nervous flight
over the white-veined surf.

A static gull coasts north.

I'm surprised by the long, various rollers,
each with a different angle of approach.

Some silent as they rise, ease in,
while a few crash loudly, shaking the cliff
 where I stand.

Still others break too soon, hissing into sand;
all relentlessly bound home,
singing as they come.

Ocean Rooms

The moon trawled the low tide far back behind the beach,
      beyond black rocks, into a shimmer of gravel

& beach glass: a Klimt rug of green, amber, gold,
      hidden most of the year in the ocean's backroom.

But it's winter solstice & a large winter sun is all chilled
      radiance this morning. The tourists are gone,

the locals still asleep or on their way to work, so the ocean
      throws open its rooms for me alone, lays bare

a million splinters & shattered deaths: shells & boats
      & glass & bones, letting the sun stun them

with air & light. All of this such wonder & wreckage,
      unburied alive between sky & sea.

I'm glad for this beach, glad for its tides, for things
      that do come back.

Just as I leave—coming close so eagerly—
      a back-lit wave swells, rises, curls, &

drowns this instant back into its kelp-choked rooms.

History Lesson

90 million years ago the sea was 600 feet higher
than it is tonight. No frost in the garden
to turn the avocados black and waxy,
to expose the thorns between each rose.
Sandy beaches stretched the length of Chile.
You could paddle to Greenland in 3 days.

But years of rain and heat
made choosing a vacation destination difficult.
A grief of storms accrued. And giant birds,
large as Lamborghinis, crossed continents of solitude
without a flap of their wings, riding the pre-nuclear,
Vulcan winds months at a time
confident the tides would change.

Sailing

Seeing the ocean
Oh, to sail on that water
to glide on her skin

Fresh Breeze

As the fresh breeze saturates the air
May it wash away all iniquity
This breeze, blowing gently
May it calm all the raging oceans.

May the breeze signal enlightenment
This breeze marking a silver lining
Ushering in optimism
What a silver lining!

As the fresh breeze permeates
May all misconceptions be gone
May all the ignorance be gone
May all the prejudice be gone
May all the hatred be gone.

Fresh and gentle breeze
Usher in effervescence
Empathy
Hope
Love
Peace
Togetherness
Tolerance
Usher in Peace for humanity.

III.

FROM ALL ANGLES

POEMS ABOUT MEMORIES, IMAGININGS, BELONGINGS & AGING

Sheltering in Santa Barbara

—April 2020

A sprinkling of sour grass
along the green hillsides,
the red-hot pokers flowering again—
yellow bursting into flame.

My daughter, home from college
in New York, types gamely
on her laptop: freshman year
could have been much worse.

My wife passes the time
strumming her guitar,
while out back I watch
the turkey vultures circle.

When the wind blows
hot in the late afternoon,
they whip against the blue sky
like a scatter of burnt embers.

Robert's Keys

       Silver—a gleam on the corner of Constance & State
yesterday—I picked up three keys,
                Robert printed on a tiny dog tag.

What woman once chose his name, as she stroked
her pregnant belly—& who whispers
                his name to him today?

I walk, at low tide, along this mussel-gleamed, breeze-
stroked beach. His keys in my hand.
                They will never open anything for me.

••

       Because they belonged to others & because I will never
know their story, I pick up
                buttons, gloves, ticket stubs—

consoled by owning some small thing from other lives & be
linked to them—as I belong
                to their brief glint here, to their dying.

••

Those keys now against my skin for an instant of impossible
intimacy, no one here to see me:
                an old woman who mourns still, paces

a beach, useless keys in fist, as waves open &
            lock their large doors as
she hums a small song to herself, almost happy.

Micheltorena and San Andres

St. Marks' in Venice has its dueling orchestras—
what passes for a business crossroads
on the savory westside of my town

has dueling planchas you can practically smell
sizzle each morning, firing up chiles
for a day of salsas, roasting onions

clear of their tears. In pots steaming
meats made of cuts my mother never
faced cellophaned at her supermarket

one finds a land where jelled and tasty
don't need a translator to dance.
Sure, in spring I awake with jasmine

pungent outside my bedroom,
almost too much, like a pre-teen
over-doused in his dad's cologne.

But I opt to run, loving the few blocks
away where my neighborhood
will hold me tight like a tortilla

that the one spot's best cook never
fails to leave on the grill to warm,
to let its secret scents out to all.

Driving Up State Street at Night:
Christmas, Santa Barbara, 1955

We stop at the light on 101, turn right up State and
pull over to the curb ... my father shifts the Hydramatic
of our shell-white Pontiac into Park, and the glowing orange
moon of the cigarette lighter rises from the dash
as my parents light-up their KENTs ....

                                              I lean over
the middle of the wide front seat to gaze at the arc
of decorations, the air sparkling for as far as I can see—
ice-colored stars and golden bells, red wreaths hanging
from each street lamp—and soon we begin swerving
around the wide white bases of 20 foot Christmas trees
stationed in the middle of the street.

                                          Last week before
Christmas, and all the shops are open until 9:00, sidewalks
packed, cars jamming all four lanes. There's OTTS
with electric trains circling in and out of *papier maché*
Swiss Alps, a display of baseball gloves and bats—
The White House where we buy my school uniforms
the color of the sea. To the right, De la Guerra Plaza
with blue, red, orange, and green bulbs strung between
the palms, and the bright office of Western Union
where I once cut my chin on the marble counter top.
Carrillo Street, Silverwoods on the corner where
my father's sport coats come from, a glow beneath
the Florsheim shoes ... then the house-high windows
of Woolworths, our station wagon reflecting in them
as we stop at the signal, and I. Magnin where I sit
on the one chair while my mother looks at the new

beige fashions. We pass the smoky haze of Pelch & Sons,
the boxes of panatellas glistening behind the glass.
I look out the back window to the tall Balboa Building
where my father reads the evening news on KTMS;
I point to a gleaming blue Cadillac gliding by.
At Anapamu "Silver Bells" by the McGuire Sisters
is piped through speakers at the base of a tree,
and diners in line at the Copper Coffee Pot move slowly
in a glimmering hive. Neon shimmers on the marquee
of the Granada Theater, and the spire of the Fox Arlington,
where I saw *Peter Pan*, disappears into the stars...
three of us, in the calm dark of the car, surrounded
by all the light it seemed the world would ever need.

Intersections

Inspired by Pablo Neruda's A Dream of Trains

"The trains were dreaming..."
of thrum and clang
whistle brass cry spilling
behind

of lull and roll
plumes of exhaust
landscapes blurring earthen paint-spill
across sunlit glass

of cigar smoke, crimson satin heels
8-year-olds reciting hymns
elderly judges snoring in rhythm
furtive replies to "Where're you headin'?"
as if it mattered

of what slips between anticipation and wool cushions
        red checker pieces
a grey worn glove
an address on a napkin

        the trains were dreaming
of wind plains
missed intersections
suitcases stored above the soul below
of tickets clutched between fingertip
and lifeline hastening
someone
somewhere
        towards morning

Blessings Upon Water

Orthodox Christmas, Santa Barbara Harbor

Late afternoon,
squads of brown pelicans soar
through golden cloud chalices.

Far below, black-robed priests
bless at least a hundred of their human flock
standing beneath the Yacht Club's pilings.

I'm arrested by the spectacle—
reminded of when I lived on Venice Beach,
took my morning coffee to the roof of my apartment,

looked toward the sea and saw, as if a dream,
full grown elephants running in the surf.
Here, the ceremony is just beginning.

Congregants follow full-bearded clergy until—
reaching the ocean's lip—silver crosses,
the size of boomerangs, are flung

into briny waves. Young boys plunge after,
dusky bodies outlined in a low slant of sun.
They do this over and over, beatific smiles

on their wet faces as they return their crosses,
anticipate the next throw—blessed and beautiful
and innocent as elephants freed from the ring.

Playground

The whistles blew; adults in orange vests
Waved us into single file on the white line
Painted on the dark asphalt ground.
We wiggled around like mischievous crows
Eager to return to the game of handball or whispering.

But, inside: I loved the number game
And writing poems loose of rhyming
We even strung together paper cranes
With strings and beads. For afternoons on end,
We sat in desks to make perfectly messy colorful folds.

And, in the end, we waited under the big
Magnolia tree for our ride to swing
Along the curb—one time I was unbuckled
In the morning and a police officer
On a motorcycle hurried after us.

I used to collect the narrow red seeds
That drop from the pods of the tree
In a plastic bag, but it became infested
With white creepy-crawlies.

Remember when you got your splinter?

A time has passed, but when no one's watching, let's go again
Above the wood chips boxed in ledge—
Belly on the black swing set—

The feet go zoom! And the world's spinning!
Spun from the sand, the air, the grass, the obstacle course,
The trees and shade where we congregated,
The top of the slide where we whispered ever more so, and
The bounce of a ball that bounced from you to me to him to her.

Murals forever painted on the wall
Yet the lines of chalk are fading.
The world is spinning in a different way.

My Grandson's Visit to Santa Barbara

Bradley's breath
and fingerprints
translucent
on my French doors
since Easter

I keep urging myself
to wash off his breath,
left on the glass
just at the height of his
three-year-old mouth.

Three weeks now
and I haven't touched
the Windex.

Bradley restless from
chocolate bunnies
my flashlight on the
floor between
uneven mattresses
as he offers me his stuffed toy.
I comfort him in the now
dark living room.
So close we close our eyes

and float   apart.

Family Soup

At the stove, cooking the kind of soup
swimming with leftovers,
my grandson, recently turned five, asks,
"How long will you survive?"

Startled, I choke, aim for simplicity.
"A long time."

"Will you live to 100?"

"Maybe." He brushes away my kiss,
pulls a toy sword from its sheath.

His older sister plays *Twinkle Twinkle Little Star*
on the piano. The oldest, age ten, informs us
she's going to college in "Glasglow"
to become a wizard like Harry Potter.

Some days you can't help standing still
in a world that will let go of you, like it
or not. For now there's a meal to serve.

"When's 100?" he continues, his sword
in the pungent air. "Almost never," I assure
to calm concern. Ask if he will sample
the soup, does it need more spice?

He likes that word, besides
he wants to be a chef. He slurps
from a spoon. "Good!" and runs off
to slay some lurking dragon.

Searching for My Own Body

My body is an old relic, archaeological dig,
the storehouse of hidden memories.
It's from the 1950s, time of black-and-white TV,
Sara Lee Pound cake, Wonder White bread
sitting on the curb eating Dixie cups in the summer;
call it innocent and carefree, suntanned without worries.
My body is a cauldron of hormones
and surprises in the making,
a bud, a blossom, a fruit about to be picked,
Hulu hooping sideshow.
My body is a tower, tallest in the school
it stands up, *Proud Mary*, *Dancing in the Streets*
then slumps. Body is a traffic light from green to red,
the green again, a rising tree, a bent limb,
a highway out of town.
It is from the 60's, a kaleidoscope,
a mud-sliding colliding charismatic *Foxy Lady*,
it's a *Locomotion*, *Hully-Gully*, *Rolling Stone*;
it's the Age of Aquarius, long haired, bare breasted
festival of senses.
It's from the 70s, a cave, a back trail, a garden
a ship at sea, hot-bed of lovemaking,
a flourish, a Fragrant Cloud rose.
In the 80 it's a deep well, wise counsel, a cow,
the fertile ground, incubator, person-maker,
Mother goddess-gateway to life and death,
bloody but unbowed.
In the 90s it's an unending worker bee,
a Mama bear, its own canyon and country. Dialect.
It is centennial, hidden hot spring, wildfire

a river flowing to the ocean,
memory keeper, archive of longing
encyclopedia of gestures.
Decades pass, a church without walls,
prayer flag flapping in the wind,
the next storm coming.
It's from now, chosen mourner,
old crow, border crosser,
protester, dreamer
a stone under the open sky
absorbing moonlight.

Social Distancing

The Monarchs seem not to have heard
of Covid-19, I think this April,
the few appearing in our backyard
sentient non-Sapiens in the navel
orange branches. We only seem alike,
liberated by sun. Locked down, we envy
their brief spring flirting with the garden shrike
among white blossoms posed like bridesmaids' posies.
For us, knowledge of good and evil
weigh down, weight turning to adipose
tissue with each generation still
taller, thickening. Even the thin are obese
next to these Monarchs in their airwaves
unweighted by knowledge of extinction.
Wingspans inches smaller than when gold-black air
first flashed me, they keep social distance to stave
off heavy-bellied sentients, blessed distance that bears
both lardy lolling and variegation.

Alive

In a bubble the size of a stadium, it's just dusk. Emergency lights bounce off the fireman's coat. I stand next to him and notice my reflection in his eyes. He looks from crumpled-up car to me and asks "You are refusing an ambulance?"

I know I am in an altered state; the impact was sudden. Events have slowed, and part of me is aware that time has shifted into a lower gear, or different gear, or all gears operating simultaneously. Around the crash scene my bubble-stadium puffs out like a sail catching wind. Through my skin and pulse I perceive, but cannot quite understand, how time is corporeal; our bodily sensations inform us of time's horizontalness.

It took 2 seconds to realize the car flying towards me was really flying towards me. My car is toast, it looks like a soda can that's been crushed by a giant boot, and surprisingly, I am OK, although my mind is blown, and it's very strange that I can feel the bubble of space we are in, and I believe it has something to do with time, and my prior concept of time has dissolved and in its place is this shifting/breathing shape of here/now, like a giant lung we are inside of, the present ripped open, yes! it's a gift! though I do not wish this sort of trauma on anyone, but everything is possible, right now, like the place Emily Dickinson dwells, and I fall in love with the fireman when he asks "You are refusing an ambulance?" I say, "I am walking and talking! I am alive!" And then I laugh. And then he laughs.

Dentist

Gracefully navigating,
Detoxifying the landscape,
Removing the impurities,
Extracting the afflicted.

In-laying the foundation
For a bright future,
Building bridges
For safety,
Drilling holes,
Filling fissures with ore.

Implanting peace subcutaneously,
Rooting canals
To feed the glutton.

Whitening the tools—
A smile to life in perpetuity.

A true healer,
An angel in disguise,
A dentist.

The Waiting Room

At least there's *People* magazine, some movie star
or British Royal on the cover. Looking for gloss,
it's Queen Elizabeth waving from under a hat
the size of a brood hen. She's been on my mind
since she addressed her subjects during the pandemic.
Her dress was the color of scrubs, a matching brooch
mounted on bosom, and the familiar pearls
she wears for pomp and doleful occasions.

In 1940, before I was born, the 14 year-old Lilybet
broadcast words of comfort to all of England's children,
especially those like herself separated for safety
from their parents during the London Blitz. I watched
her coronation on our grainy black and white Philco
sandwiched between my parents and brothers.
Mom was pregnant with our third brother on the way.
We pressed our noses so close to the screen,
Dad said we'd all go blind. All that's left of our family
is my little brother and me. He finally watched the crowning
on his TV starring an actress who looked nothing like the Queen.

The Queen and I have grown old together, worn our share
of ridiculous fashion. During COVID, her message
seemed to include the whole frightened world. *We shall endure,*
she told us, one hand on a writing desk, steady eyes on ours.
We will be with our families again, she said. *We will meet again,*
she promised. Who are we to doubt the Queen of England?

Waiting

I have not seen the images that fortell this child to be
held snugly in the womb until the time is right to set her free
But I've been told that she will be with us in winter
and so I think of her mother, fragile as a pink lily
sepals of fine hair brushed into a spikey-do, snug
in her papa's sinewy arms, an earlier child of winter.

Unable to penetrate her life, now in a far northern place
I imagine her, regal, tossing her mane of fiery red hair
as she hurries to the market to buy a fish to nurture
the tiny creature swimming under her heart
waiting for her time, the birthing hour when blue white milk
will replace the forces that now pump nutrients into her child.

The Kings River

For my mother, La Verne

The Kings River
flowed
through your veins,
            you insisted;
the pomegranate
and the liquidambar you
planted years before
rooted in your bones.

            Now I understand.

You rest with that oak,
half a millennium old
its roots in the icy
Sierra runoff.

It sings
of the sycamores'
loves and the heartbreak
of the river

and you remember your own

Sporty Girl

I wish I could say I was the kind of child who
was sporty, fearlessly hurling herself over a vault,
cartwheeling across the lawn, hitting a homerun—
hitting the ball at all might be worth saying.

I did get a Sharpshooter Rifle blue ribbon at sleep-away camp.
I wish I could tell you why I was so strangely good at that.

I wish I could say I walked the long seashore,
enchanted by the sound of waves, or hid deep
in the dense woods of New York under moonlight
as if it were my private world, as if called to it.

But my bedroom was the ticket, dancing to my 45s
the exercise, drawing and writing at my desk
the nature I traversed, reading books like a sport.

Bobbsey Twins on first base,
Black Beauty on second, *The Snow Goose* on third,
Emily Dickinson back at home plate.

I was Captain of my bedroom, my team—a solo affair.
I could hurl myself into imagination
and win first place.

Faces

Taos, NM 2009

They say that you belong here
only if you can see the face
of Taos Mountain so every day I look
but do not belong.

In front of me in the checkout line
stands a man, solid and strong
but his stiff side won't bend
won't allow him to lift

the groceries he's pushed this far
so I say to him *I can help*
and he turns to me
though I can see
that even this motion
strains him

as he whispers *thank you.*
In his face I see
bald, burned patches of combat,
wildfires on the ridge.
I see
the face of a mountain.

Someday

They say someday we'll live on Mars
And visit moons like touring czars
Collecting comet tails in jars.
That all is fine with me.

But I think that a cup of tea
At one small cafe by the sea
With your bright hair blown wild and free
Would send me to the stars.

House

In the slip of a season, doors
slink from hinges, damp rot wins.

Mother's house hitches as vines grow
into its eyes. I harvest its parts:

doorknobs and bricks, the arched
window through which we glimpsed

the wolf and long night moons.
The walls—I commit to thorn,

let oaks root in the rotted floor,
lichen and moss riot.

In forty years, a blossom,
revenant from her lily bank, might stop

a hunter in his tracks. He will lower
        the gun, but not know why.

Old Pillow

So flattened by weight, gravity
or loss of down or foam
it lay beneath my head no

softer than ground, so many
decades of seeing me to sleep
or not, toward good dreams

or nightmares or my hours
turning over days like compost
piles, all those nights becoming

many miles of a life so unsettled
it kept me awake half of the time.
Still, to me it was sublime, smell

taking me all the way back to my
college days & maybe even beyond
that, to boyhood, not best of times,

barely tolerable, yet I clung
to it as if it was something
loved. My older neck ached

for something comforting,
sleep-inducing, tuned to a
life I had grown into. I got us

both new pillows. You traded up,

while I put mine on top of the one
I might have left behind, replaced

but not gone, ghost-ground, so
slight in the way of padding for
these fewer years I had ahead.

A Single Chair

To test what
singleness can bear,
yesterday I saw
a chair, *FREE*,
on the curb
and hauled it
to my lair.
The skirt had just
one little tear.
It could rock and
twirl and raise
my feet into the air.
Perfect, the way
my body fit
with just a bit of
room to spare.
Easy not to care if
spiders left
their webs or
sacks of eggs.
It was a dare
and only fair to
have my own
comfort-chair--
not like a pair
I had to share
with anyone who
entered there.
My room with just
its single chair.

Green Heels

Sweet little cloth-covered pumps
      in emerald silk about size five
   stored in a cedar chest for 50 years or more,
preserved for their charm
      (sinuous straps with a platform sole).
   A tiny woman spinning

into some long gone night,
      such special shoes, vanity afoot.
   My mother's, small woman of
modest desires—but the shoes
      tell a different story—
   party girl, lover of the dance,

the quick step and twirl, a hot hand
      at the waist, slippery nylons
   and a garter belt, fox-trotting and
jitterbugging, dance hall men, the night
      as long as it needed to be.
   Those high-stepping shoes

saved through move after move,
      growing children and dawning
   troubles, tucked into a trunk until
the errant daughter left them out,
      so careless. The long, sweet story
   of the steps they made eaten by the dog.

Ode to Bob the Shoe Man

Bob lifts me by my armpits
onto a tiny couch, upholstered
in slick, cherry-red vinyl with fine
glitter beneath the surface, like the
backseat of a custom T-Bird.

He sets my foot on a chilly metal
scale and runs the thingy up and down
my inner arch. I giggle, but Bob
is all business, a doctor of little feet.
You're growing fast, kiddo.

He dashes a note to himself, slips
the pencil behind his ear, and disappears
through a curtain to THE BACK ROOM,
where beautiful shoes await. My mother
browses nearby, while I meld to vinyl

and watch for that curtain to stir, dizzy
on epoxy-polish-saddle-soap-tanning-oil.
Did the curtain move? Did it? Just as
I'm about to give up, Bob emerges, deftly
balancing a tower of pastel boxes.

Now I am six. I sit in a kiddy chair.
Feet that wear saddle shoes get all
wiggly over Keds in Spring colors.
Bob opens each box, teases the tissue
like it might hold the shoe of my

dreams. Now I am twelve, taller
than the boys, big feet like a pup.
Bob watches me moon over a pair
of size fives. I think, *My feet will grow
forever. I will crush tall buildings,*

like Godzilla. The Shoe Man knows
just what to say, and who to say it to:
When we want to model our ladies' shoes,
he confides, leaning toward my mother,
we look for long, graceful feet, like hers.

Andirons

A pair of andirons
flanking the door
might have served
as a warning—

literal and blunt,
to say the whole house
was a fire box,
a place of cinders.

Or the meteor, a livid flame
that blistered across the sky
long enough to wish upon
had I not been so amazed,

might have implied
a pyric calamity
if I were given
to reading signs.

as it is
I am not.

I thought them
only coincidental
to the brush
the heat and the wind

and so we moved in
and spread our books around
and laid down our bed
and for one week

we lived there,
oblivious to the augury
of iron and stars
and even common sense.

Only in the last hour
a blaring incendiary wind
kindled sign and sense
in me

and flared to the foretold and inevitable.
So that when the fire came
I had always known
it would.

Forecast

The storm I sent for you walks
on the tips of the pines.

Still visible from space
because the light bulbs are different,
the divide between East and West Berlin
is a kind of Milky Way
for lost agrarian planes.

The rain first is heard,
then felt. A figure
in the red truck
between the tall firs.
It has not come for your
suitcase with the straps.

I never took off the tiny
glove from that winter.
I grew up.

My hand squeezing the memory
still the hand of a little girl.

Notes for an Oil Painting:

Driving south to L.A., colors fade
as yawning light drenches the landscape

Greens receded to grays

Rounding a curve, a row of taillights
define the side of mountain

A silver train, tilting, strains the track,
rumbling past

While the distant city glows hills into
flat shadows as we speed into night's
dark palette

Inverted Root

i am going to make something
of this day

be still   concentrate
on the hands

each transition
each grace note

the sharp-less mode
the inverted root

there is much
rephrasing

each verse is a place
to spend the night

Open Mic

One thinks poetry's a couch
to make the world play therapist,
or at least take note and listen.

One thinks poetry's a prayer book,
calling the faithful to litany
or the faithless to become congregation.

One thinks poetry's a weapon
to shoot the head with images of war
or blast away the combat's trauma.

One thinks poetry's a bullfrog,
shut in a shoebox, ready to croak
or jump out inappropriately during show and tell.

One thinks poetry's a vase
to preserve cuttings from the garden
or store stony trinkets collected from private shores.

One thinks poetry's confetti,
empty color tossed haphazardly,
or blinding shards thrown like glitter into the eyes.

One thinks poetry's a jar of formaldehyde
to display pale, shriveled organs
or the internal parasites that feed upon them.

One wonders if poetry deserves the polite applause
it receives at this event for its presentation
or if the art has been lost
at the hands of these practitioners.

An Abundance of Tears

From an article on crying, I learn
that crying has health benefits
I am drawn to such information
as I am a world class crybaby

Show me a returning dad in uniform
surprising his seven year old child
at a school assembly, or a little
boy getting the puppy he longed for
as a birthday gift. Let me hear a ravishing
glissando on the piano and I will weep

Bring me your special needs prom queens
poignant episodes of Downton Abbey
a gaunt animal rescued by kind strangers
a soprano aria spun like liquid silver
and a lump will rise in my throat
My eyes burn, my vision blurs

Based on a careful reading of the essay
I am pleased to learn that crying soothes
relieves pain, releases hormones
that enhance mood, calms stress
fights bacteria in the eye, and
improves vision by keeping the eyes moist

So, bring on the last three uplifting minutes
of David Muir's evening newscast
showing an eight year old selling lemonade

to help buy a wheelchair for his friend
or 94 year old President Carter with a black eye
stiches on his forehead, smiling, hammer in hand
building houses for Habitat for Humanity
one day after falling at his home in Georgia
Show me anything like that, and spontaneously
I do my level best to maintain my health!

Conversing Under Fresco

The architecture más grande is above our heads
when we learn that, yes, perfect symmetry is possible.

The builders, the Greeks, flourished when ships of foreigners
came and traded their wits, science, and languages.

So why not use another language to describe everyday
concepts like the color blue, because then we discover

in Russian, light blue and dark blue are completely different; in English,
we simply have blue; and ancient Greeks had no word for it at all.

We know blue inspires peace
and confidence, which we need in our daily lives. Habitual,

like drinking water, feeling sunlight, and
hearing birds chirp at day and crickets chirp

at night, we are quiet, but some parts of the world
are loud and widely open to sing, dance, and drink

with the whole-heartedness of knowing that
this is a good time. Cups clink and

eyes and teeth are shining. Wherever we are—

     amidst arches & curves

          the intricacy within the fresco

living & celebrating.

The Blue Poet

A brown umbrella
stippled with rain drops

sings to the blue poet
in the green glade

her thoughts a whirl
beside the tumbling brook

one white calla bent
to the day falling

away from itself
without end

Together for a Future Generation

We are a generation
Yearning for peace and harmony
We are that generation
Pleading for togetherness.

We are that generation
Longing for fairness
A resolute generation
Determined to uphold Dr. Martin Luther King's dream
A generation longing for togetherness.
A generation nostalgic to live Dr. King's dream
A dream calling for togetherness and justice
We plead for one nation
A nation where content of character is judged, not skin color.

We are that generation aching for togetherness
Working together like a swarm of bees
Hate will only bring us all down
Divided the world retrogresses
Imagine a troubled, divided, loveless world!

We are a generation aching for equality and unanimity.
Our world can prosper
If we work together
Work together in harmony

We are an aching generation
Aching to uplift one another
Support each other

Love one another
Stand up and plead for a better future
A brighter future for all generations.

Let Dr. King's dream come to fruition
As we stand and work together
Working together like a swarm of bees
As we work together,
We prosper
Peace, justice, and equality prevails
Together we build a brighter tomorrow
Working as one we empower future generations

Hear our generation as we cry for togetherness
Divided we languish in a gloomy abyss
Together we soar like an eagle
We glide high in the winds of success.

What is left

when the blues knock out all your conviction
is the clink of a cup set to table,
slush of sweet tea poured from kettle to vessel,
creak of old wood as you sit in the chair,
and your hand. Your loyal hand knows how
to write essential tasks, order the day.
Remember to pick up butter, eggs, milk.
Make pumpkin muffins for Pat and Celeste.
Do breathing exercises 3x at least.
The ink scrolls out a rhythm, you see
there's time enough to honor every moment
and it's OK, for now, to go at it slow.
Today is who you have become, just this.
You survive. Quietly, you start to sing.

if something should happen

for instance, if plates,
                    tectonic I mean, should
                                    shift under all that weight
                    between them, cause earth
to fall into itself &
                    take everything with it, if roof
                                    above my head should
                    fall, leaving only stars
&, tonight a moon we call
                    thumbnail, if ground
                                    opens to swallow whole
                    what until now we've found
stable, will I know
                    to stand up from the table
                                    where I've just served dinner
                    & offer a toast to life,
find the right rhyme in
                    that moment of dissolution,
                                    say, *l'chaim* to each guest
                    I've ever invited in, all
of us toasting with unbroken
                    glasses, by which I mean,
                                    hearts, as we fall, face-first
                    into the next place?

The Secret of Longevity

According to Ruby Lee Markham, dead today
in North Carolina at age one hundred
and twelve: Invest as little
in this world as possible. Fake Death out.
Make him think you couldn't give a care
whether he visits now or tomorrow morning.
Spend the forty-eight years of your retirement
reading, playing cards and solving
crossword puzzles. Watch *Jeopardy*
every night at six, and follow it
with *Wheel of Fortune*: Death dislikes routine.
Lose your spouse midway through your life—
he or she will only vex you later. Above all,
if you, too, want to be the world's
tenth oldest person, don't have any children.
While the others in the nursing home
suffer one disappointment hard
upon another—sons losing their hair
and jobs, daughters divorcing, grandchildren
gone to drugs—nod pleasantly
at their misfortune. Have a sympathetic aide
shuffle the cards, then follow the strategies
that have served you for a century: Do what you can
to get an Ace on top. Free up columns quickly
for your Kings. Cheat, if you must.

Driving Meditation

When I steer it backwards
into a curbside spot,
I know this steel skin
down to the very inch,

and while I've walked the sidewalk,
refusing words, listening
to footsteps, watching leaf
shadows wave, never

until yesterday have I
made my mind a blank
and watched the white stripes
pulse by, the cars

beside me floating in the heat.
In emptiness and stillness,
I miss my exit, lose
my way, arrive.

Silent Retreat in Texas

On the banks of the Guadalupe River,
limestone borders like butter-sticks
leave the water a dusty teal.

Only pecan trees can withstand
the frequent floods, their taproots
anchored deep, their bases wide

as tiny ships, a non-floating flotilla
in single file along the tempestuous shore,
a steady expedition sailing securely in place.

As I listen in the current stillness,
I sink down my roots too so that
I am ready for the coming storm.

A Dream

where I've lost everything
including the where and to
it's almost beautiful
how not knowing where to go
leads you to places never been.
On pure chance, it seems,
the steps lead *right here*.

So, my question is
where are these places I've never been?
I want to interrogate each one,
know its scenery, smooth roads,
as well as its inevitable bumpy ones.
Perhaps the hill that blocks my view
is hiding something precious
on the other side.

Through and through I dream
of history
as I retrace my steps, and see:

each step I've lost
a second dream

Song

something cannot happen
without hands
    i want to say
something cannot grow
    without touch
    can you hear me

somewhere is not
without hunger

    in the fields
    in the kitchen
    on a canvas
    on a page
    can you hear it

make a song
    a trench
    in the earth
    sprinkled with
    seeds

or a stave
    like a perch
    for the human voice
    through which
    arpeggios of sunlight
    ascend

Swallowed

When you lie beneath the night,
breeze a lover's breath,
darkness a relief,
stars can keep you awake.

Memories tease like ants.
The sand's too warm for sleeping.
Dim light makes shadows of trees.
The wind stops at midnight.

This is what you've been waiting for.
Now you can breathe.
Above, canyon walls grin.
Dark lips have swallowed you.

You are in and of the earth
and still alive to tell it.
If this is to be a resurrection,
you do not want to sleep.

The Book of Snacking

I like to eat almond butter and
raisin sandwiches.
There's a good reason for the word butter—
the fat content is listed at 26 percent.

Years ago, when I was
thirty pounds heavier and pre-diabetic
I promised my doctor I would lose weight and
get six-pack abs.

I told her,
I'm gonna look like
Clint Eastwood!

When I go for my annual physical I wear
shorts, a t-shirt, no socks,
get a haircut, fast for a day,
take laxatives,
skip my morning coffee.

When she measures my blood pressure
and pulse I hold my breath and visualize:

Saturday morning,
junior league at Matador Bowl.
Mom drops me off at
9 AM, gives me 35 cents

to buy a snack.
I bowl 155. The league
gives me a patch.

143 pounds, 110/60, that's great! she says,
and look at those abs!

That's enough worshiping,
I'd say.

Skinny Belt Sings the Blues

Honey I try my best to connect
　while you suck in breath and hold
　　one end of myself to the other
　　　round peg reaching for round hole
　　　　but either I've shrunk or you've expanded
　　　　　and my chic leopard self cannot curl around you
　　　　　with the old feline grace I reminisce about
　　　　　　threading myself through sleek designer jeans
　　　　　dropping lower imitating a boa
　　　　　to drape those sumptuous hips
　　　　　snug in black lycra sheath
　　　　　accentuating your curves
　　　　　with my wild spotted self
　　　　　in a full contact embrace
　　　　　so I apologize
　　　　　and grieve my inevitable transition
　　　　to the give-away pile
　　　　though I will fondly remember
　　　our time together
　　　the sweet rise and fall
　　of your breath
　　the tender way
　you eased me open
after a satisfying meal
　the reckless abandon
as you flung me to the floor
when you were eager to undress.

Hot Flash

Hot flash isn't quite right
not entirely accurate
more like a rosy dawn
spreading over my body sky
or
a crescendo of applause
breaking out in the audience
at the close of the symphony
signaling the end of the music

Old Soul

Dusk, en route to a party,
I'm lost. Roam the road's serious curves.
Address numbers grow smaller when
they should be rising. The road stops,
a mountain collapsed on its back. I turn around
as if I can reverse the order of things.
Behind a hedge, toward light, I crunch up
a gravel drive. Am greeted by a man,
his gray hair tied back in a ponytail,
grinning in the backglow. Pronounces,
You're an old soul, very old.
No wonder I'm lost.
Lincoln, you were married to him.
I ignore him, ask my psychic host
if he could tell me where to find the address
I hold out. "I don't do directions," he says.
Tells me to go back to town and start over.
Continues naming other old souls I might be—
Katharine of Aragón, Bonaparte's wife.
It's getting darker by the minute. *I know,*
Calamity Jane, he shouts as if he's hit
the jackpot. I find myself
on the back of a horse, shoot off a call
to my friend who says turn left,
not right, look for balloons
on her mailbox. I kick into high gear
beating it out of Dodge.

Birthday 70+

"You haven't changed,"
over and over I am told.
Not changed? I smile,
repeating my standard reply,
"You mean I looked over 70
when you met me so many years ago?"

I laugh at the absurdity.
Like an old house
I may look the same
on the outside,
but inside I have been remodeled.
  Eyes with new lenses,
  Ears with aids to hear,
  Even a heart, not entirely original,
   with its new valve recently installed.
My body hidden beneath layers of cloth
  a landscape of biopsies and scars.
Although my feet,
  formerly my best feature
  are now marred with bunions and callouses,
  they are still able
  to carry me into another year.

Dancing with Angels

Looking backward at ninety,
looking forward to heaven,
you're getting ready to move
out of one life-zone
into another.

You speak of death like it's the vacation you've been promised
but never taken,
like people you love are waiting there
and you're holding up the party,
like God Himself is fitting you with dancing shoes,
feet that won't hurt
and eyes that can see again.

Years ago, I remember,
'Grandmother' had too formal a sound,
so I gave you love-names
and made up songs
and stories in your honor.

I guess I still do.

What I Forgot to Remember

why did I come into this room
better backtrack my steps

talking to friends   now what is her name
better start with A

my head is in the fridge
no sunglasses in here

is today my dental appointment
oh no   was that yesterday

help   I forgot to put out the trash
or is that tomorrow

that word is on the tip of my tongue
but tucked away in my brain

bring in the dog and let out the cat
did I or didn't I

will I remember tomorrow what I forgot today
or remember today and forget tomorrow

I can't remember

Whiteout

I watch my ninety-one year old mother traverse
the aisles of Walmart in quest of the perfect white
purse. As if approaching the summit of Everest she
digs into a mountain of mark downs, zips, unzips, buckles,
unbuckles, to find one with pockets for a flip phone, two sets
of keys, three bus schedules and a rescue inhaler she refuses to use.
It must hold an address book of friends, most of whom no longer need an
address, mints, antacids, gum and a magnifying glass the size of a salad plate.
She inspects a suitcase-sized purse that opens accordion-style, compartments
for envelopes of cash labeled food, clothes, medicine as well as space for scissors,
in case her sleeve gets caught in a shopping cart. She leaves nothing to chance, finds
a purse with small sections for comb, lipstick, tweezers, and her wad of credit cards
held together with thick rubber bands. I watch as she peers into each smooth lining,
feels for a safe place to hide her rice paper wallet, the one with my father's picture glued
on the flap, the one her arthritic hands struggle to open. A purse with memory and function,
a mobile unit slung over her shoulder, rope and pickaxe for the slow, uneven climb ahead.

Biblioteca

In the off season
Commuters cross the
Stage of the 8 bit
Amphitheater
Within the immense
Emptiness some youth
In the upper rows
Talk over traffic
Typical to the
Surrounding region
For decades booming
With citrus cargo and
Construction their play
On fate private and
Immaterial

IV.

LET ME COUNT THE WAYS

POEMS ABOUT FAMILY, AFFECTION & LOVE

Cell Speaks

In singles or groups we
Always exist,
You made us,
So that
We make you,
Fifty trillions of us
Live inside you in communion,
We survive because
We love one another;
The strong empower the weak—
All is powerful,
The healthy heal the sick—
All is healthy,
Yet,
We are commanded by
Your thoughts, feelings and emotions,
So,
Send us love—
Send us kindness—
Send us compassion,
We—
Send you life.

I Imagine my Great-Great Grandfather on the Illinois and Michigan Canal

The steady hoofbeat of six draft
        horses pulling his boat south
  from Chicago to LaSalle. You'd think
their rhythm would distract him
     from the cargo that he's hauling,
        but always his mind's on *things*:
  rags and rosin, soap and sugar,
potatoes and mechanic's tools.
     Early fall. Blackberry bushes
       along the bank beginning to wither,
  the peppery smell of wet soil.
Sometimes he thinks that 1857
     will never end, that the pig iron
       and millstones weigh
  down Time itself. Fifty-pound
sacks of salt and horseshoe nails.
     Plow blades and marble and lead.
       Dawn breaks the color of broomcorn,
  and evening's golden as rum or rye.
At night, the others snoring, he lies awake
     on his bed of freight and canvas,
       staring at stars, praying for God
  to enter him ... but the closest he can get
to the Divine are smells:
  freshly-cut tobacco and vinegar,
     salted mackerel and turpentine.

Trick or Treat

Four year old Wyatt, a Sheriff in chaps, kerchief,
double pistols on his hip, instructs Willie, almost two,
a puffy green dinosaur, on the subtle magic of Halloween.
Handing Willie his plastic pumpkin with the black handle,
Wyatt pushes Willie outside the screen door, slams it shut

and says, "Say it Willie ... say Trick or Treat".
First a soft whisper, Willie struggles with "r's",
but he stays in the game, and shouts "Tick or Teet".

So begins repeat and repeat,
open the door, then shout "Trick or Treat,"
sheriff and dinosaur chant the great chant
all children must know before roaming the streets.

Wyatt takes it to heart and offers a cheer,
"Good job Willie, you can say it real clear,
they won't make you stay in the stroller this year!"

Doc, My Garden Mentor

for my grandfather

I remember the smell of earth,
the sun warming my browned body,
birds overhead, occasional visits
from ants and bees.

Today my hands knead
moist Kentucky earth, red and rich,
relying on instinct to know when
just the right texture is reached:
when soil seems to open up
and welcome a naked plant.

These hands have done that
so many times since my childhood,
first with encouragement
later on for the sheer joy of it.

And the joy of seeing my grandfather,
Doc, bent over some zucchini,
snake-like, among its vines,
like a doctor working a patient's wound,
caressing almost the pain out of it,
talking to it with his knowing touch.

"I knew it," he'd say. "See that? It's root worm."
He'd stop a moment then sever the plant,
ripe with its bounty, to protect the rest,
spray around this or that

"just to be sure." Off he'd toss
that dirt-worn beige hat
from his bald head, his forearm
would wipe the drops from his sweaty brow.
His upturned face, craggy ancient,
would grimace at the high-up sun
then turn to me and say, "Let's eat."

Really?

There are dragons in your garden
and bats inside your dreams?
The tree there by the window's filled with ghosts?
And even worse–you say
the crocodile beneath your bed
just waits to bite your toes?

We sent them all away last night,
swept them out, locked the door,
told them not to come here anymore.

Don't you remember?
Oh, you do.
They did?
I see.
A frightful state, I do agree.

Come here, my sweet, and sleep by me.

Darkness

For Kyrah

It is
hard
to be
very scared
and
be
very little
in
the
rubble
and
wait
for the
morning
that
never
comes

From the Backseat

The almond orchard she passes
on the 101 extends for miles.
Uniformed rows of tightly packed trees
are buried at their base,
parched in crumbled soil.
Thousands of shrunken trunks,
grayed with twiggy winter branches
look whimsically reversed,
as if it's their root ball atop
and someone's playing a joke.

And these passing trees...
they are still—
still as a December cemetery,
and remind her of the vast graveyard
her dad would drive by
on their way to the city.
Short white-rowed tombstones
immersed in hilly lush lawns
fluttering by her window,
a flurry of oversized index cards
she tries to count.

Each is a fallen soldier her dad says.
She doesn't believe him
and the child confidently claims
they're oversized teeth,
polished white fossils
left by long ago giants.

Her glance for his reassurance
dissolves as his solemn face
turns the stones into real men,
and her own little body
into numb disbelief.

She doesn't understand
dead men.
Men are strong and smart
and in charge.
This must be
an adult thing.
Something she'll understand later.
But she's 50 now
and still doesn't.

Question of the Day

The feet of squirrels
have worn the bark of this oak.
On the inner sides of branches
the bark's cragginess is darker, almost smooth
where light neat feet
climb for acorns, a mate,
to escape a fox. I wouldn't have
noticed this if my daughter hadn't
stopped here to ask me a question,
to pitch her resplendent often inconvenient tent
of unrushed being. Dadda, she asks, how many days
fit inside a tree? I look up to the branches.
Silver nicks of light skate up and down
strands of web. A junco, a handful
of shadow, hops along a branch
towards the top of the crown.
I repeat, careful to keep my voice straight,
How many days fit inside a tree?
Yes, she responds, yes.
I'm blind for a spell, almost afraid,
but very close to something. I look at her face.
I look at Tomasa's face, the face that of all the faces
moves me the most. How many days fit inside a tree?
I repeat again. That's a very good question. Then I answer.
I answer with a final gentle certitude. One million.
One million? Yes, I say. One million exactly.

A Box of Old Photos

This is the closest I'll get to you, old man,
now that you're gone—these old photos
develop new meaning.

There will be no more new memories,
even those I have continue
                              to fade.

How vain to think I can hold on
to the afternoon musk of tobacco sweat &
labor my hands have never known.

The ice blue of your eyes aged kindly,
how your words tumbled like stones
softened with years—

now when I look at you I see
into the past but cannot return to tell you
all those things a grown son sees.

The Life Force

Mother, until the end
  impeccably dressed,
      having chosen from among her two hundred pairs of shoes
      with a matching purse,
      lining the walls of closets,
      filled with a multitude of stylish clothes.

Mother, until the end
  coiffed and manicured,
      red hair and nails,
      reflecting her passion for living.
Mother, until the end
  vital and vivacious,
      energetically running
      to luncheons and dinners,
      movies and plays,
      Mahjong and bingo.
Mother, until the end
  loving and loved.

The Life Force
      born with us
      taken for granted,
      source of strength,
      fired by genetics, lifestyle and luck.
The Life Force
      a miracle fuel,
      burning itself out—slowly
      getting us ready
      to sleep forever.

Mother, in the end
      beautiful, but withered,
      undressed, without shoes,
      listless and tired,
      laying and waiting,
      confused and silent,
      dependent and incapable,
Mother, in the end,
      cared for with love.

Haiku for Bill Lanphar

Oh, our dear brother
Silent steel strings sing no more
A still water now

Red Horse

Navajo Nation

His last day an old man whittles
wood for his grandson, conjures
a horse from a chunk of high desert, stains
its coat mesa-red, speckles its back like a pheasant's,
adds a bit of hair for mane and tail,
gives it to the child who now holds in his hand

this horse shaped by his grandfather's hand
and he slips out early, this boy,
and finds you, Red Horse, as if his grandfather's
gift had brought you, waiting
on the freshly powdered plain, your hooves
printing haloes on the ice. The boy climbs
on your back, one hand still clutching

the wooden horse. With a moss-soft
nicker you carry him through juniper,
ponderosas. Staring up at the trees,
the boys thinks, *tall, like horses.* He hears
a blueblack herd gallop through the clouds,
sees shadows hover in the shape of horses,
even pinyon smoke, to this boy, is scented
like horses. You take him through canyons
to the family's sheep, a good ride, and he knows

that when he grows older and goes to places
you are not, Red Horse, to strange places
where this place is not, he will keep close
the wooden horse, your likeness shaped
by his grandfather's hand, that he might call you
to lead him home.

Theory of Happiness

He dreamed a melancholy song
called "When Will I Be Happy?"

The melody descended on a minor scale
and the lines rhymed like doors

in a corridor shutting one by one.
Thunder and wonder, listen and glisten,

tears and mirrors, falling and stalling.
In the soft soprano voice, he found

one kind of happiness.

Jacaranda petals on the car's hood.
Summer sweat and melting ice cream.

First flakes of snow blowing
through the cobblestone street.

Refusing the if only. Rejecting
that's when. Finding it now,

in the listen, in the glisten,
in the wonder and thunder.

If I Wrote A Poem

It would praise the smooth grey boulders
I climbed in Central Park when I fled there
after school—the view they gave of people
prone on blankets on the lawn. Squirrels
on their haunches weighing if I was beast
or doe. Without backs turned away at home
reminding me what I was and wasn't,
the chain mail vest I'd hitched around
my chest slipped off. Essence of willow oak
and sassafras and silverbell rushed in
a different form of love. I could see the hundred
kinds of trees that framed the sky—a million
hands nearly touching but not blocking
each other's sun.

May Mother Earth Forgive Me

despite my inhibitions.
i find myself willing

(desperate, craving, ever so pliable)

to fell redwoods in your name,
to melt icebergs and drain oceans,
all to feel your patient smile

(as it gently warms the earth i stand upon)

heal the damage i've torn.

if only i could etch
half my love for you into my bones
(words as eternal as the gaping maw of soil and fungi allow)
and send the other half to the stars.

(for only the infinite and knowing cosmos could truly understand my
truest devotion towards you.)

Delira

—Honoring those lost in Haiti on January 12, 2010

like Delira
you plunged
your hand into the dirt
you stopped
you returned the dirt to the earth

4 times you bent
picked up loose soil
and let the fine powder
go through your long fingers

yon pongnen, a handful
for your grandmother
one for your mother
one for your daughter
one pinch for the daughter of your daughter
all gone that day

you implore
and commit their souls
mother earth
they are yours to guard!

Sonnet for Mark

Now wakes a path between the oaks, now
falls a spell of dove and frog, and stones
dream of their mountain clans and each stick
breaks to hear its name. Now light edges creek
and water appears as a quick coin trick or
silk pulled from a funnel of months, now
behind us, at last, and shade and sky fill
the mirror moving from next to next. Now
do you see there is no stillness to this world?
Even in sleep a seed is knitting its breach
from the dark and the body hums
on the march to becoming less and right
now, words depart then arrive, like a brush
returning to a well of color.

Most Importantly, That

Amazed in waves by the world,
agog how simple it is to create,
from nothing, an apple. It's just seed
and time, water, sun, and soil.
After a few years, the blossoms,
the bees, and the small fruit.
How little it took for this majesty
to be here, scattering the ground
with fruit, the air scented with cider,
and inside the house, you love me.

Pandemic Domestic

When a week into a daily month
of poems the inspiration cupboard
seems bare, consider the sofa
in the other room, the wired fireplace,

cheery, fake and smoke-free,
all the better in this ailing age when
one cough can send the mind
reeling. Sit there with the wife

you never could have imagined
and who is somehow yours, even if
that's too possessive for what
you've managed to build between.

Screw words, so many mean
different things, the synonyms
and antonyms piling up like logs
you can't burn in the electric fire.

There's nothing but to hold, hold on.

Not-Knowing

Write about curiosity
about how not-knowing
motivates the mind.
Overlook advice that
urges you to have
all the answers.
Find a way to keep
living the questions—
Rilke said that.

Reach for some star
that manages to shine
through the darkness.
Curl into the circle
of friends.
Do it often.

Ignore the spun-out
parts of you.
Sit in the sun.

Don't overlook
the listener who has time
to linger on the bank of
time's fast-moving river.

Learn to swim.
It's ok if you don't
do it well. Just enough
to get you to safety.

Remember safety.
Hear it whisper
your name.

For Doctor Emmerson on the Occasion of My New Hip

I'm writing this poem for my surgeon
since I don't raise backyard chickens
so cannot give him a basket
filled with avian bonbons tied with a ribbon.

I'm writing this poem for my surgeon
because I can't afford the latest phone.
And much as I'd like, I'm unable to gift him
a week on an island I happen to own.

So I'm writing this poem
to remember my joy
when I slept through the night,
pain gone.

I'm writing this poem to say
I am grateful,
ever grateful, to you,
Doctor Emmerson.

My Heart Broke Loose with the Wind

(In response to: "Poetry" by Pablo Neruda)

On the pages of a Khalil Gibran journal
my voice was freed—the wind squalled
through my brain beaten
down by words, abusive.

Such liberation possessed me wholly.
His revelation bloomed,
so unlike my mother's mutterings
as she drifted in and out of madness.

My lines, at ten, engendered
many other poems holding and healing
me—once so deeply shattered.
Those words now yearning for the divine
just like the prophet Khalil Gibran.

Blue

Atmospheric haze scatters sunlight's opalescence
into waves of azure, cornflower, hyacinth.

Those who've left us are dispersed in clouds of dust,
remnants of breath, our planet's exhalations.

You, my friend, are closer now to sky,
almost relieved of gravity, emptied of darkness,

as if indigo had surrendered itself
to dawn.

MV Conception

There's a hole in the harbor
A hole in my heart
An ocean of tears can't fill

Missing You

You have put the black leaves
in the red teapot
but you are gone.

The place where you slept
is wide with your body
but there is no warmth.

You are in the garden
chopping the Mexican marigold
creosote smell cloaking the roses.

Or you are walking the blue hills
behind the house
hills older than all walking.

Outside the window the almond tree
is a white trembling
blossoms drifting from the parted buds.

You are gone and the day is wide
as the ocean
and as merciless.

There is no season for this waiting
heart flexed
the long breath of return.

Another Recipe for Getting Lost

I often go walking in places I normally don't
because I expect you might be there.
Your heavy hat erasing your eyebrows
and the ridiculous cravat of rolled musical papers
you hold so close.

The grandpa over there cannot stop
clapping and singing for the grandson's picture
even after it's too late and the boy
has crossed the ocean.

The birds have their own traffic lights
for walking across the lawn.

Le Carrousel's tra-la-la
moves even the riderless horses.
One of them has a really long mane,
which is confused when the whole thing
up and turns.
It doesn't know whether to trail in a circle
or stick out behind straight as a beam.

His Smile

In response to "Your Laughter" by Pablo Neruda

Take my diamonds, bury my treasures
and burn my books, but *never*
take away your smile.

Don't take back the carnation you picked
as a child, the baby food left on porcelain plates
or that golden light on everything
on the day you were born, son.

Your sadness—each day of it—
pools into the lining of me: those many worlds
on your brow and in your gaze's shadow.

Let me tug them from you as you sleep
not far from the turbulent ocean:
such mystery and regret.

I smile at you.
You didn't smile back then.
But you do, now.
I walk away, glowing.

Tandem

At the weary turn a young couple flies down our mountain
on a bicycle-built-for-two—all speed and grace and glory.

They lean into the hairpin in perfect synchrony
her golden hair a flag flying for the nation of youth,

helmets not required in a place they'll live forever.
Damn their youth and beauty!

They make it look so easy—falling in love, while not falling
Remember falling? We rode tandem—*once*.

Newlywed, and the lake path unfurled like a satin ribbon.

you peddled
       I braked
           I pedaled
               you braked
                    the bike wobbled
                         and lurched

always on the edge of falling, and oh my heart leaping everywhere!

If strangers had been watching we were unaware. Nothing pretty
about our off-kilter rhythm, but it carried us through forty years

into this bewildering country of wheelchairs and loss, encroaching
gravestones everywhere, our rhythm now

           honed and steady
          steady and honed
            me pushing
               you letting go.

Twin Souls

He places the two soles
of her discarded sandals together.

The stitched outlines
mirror as they sit across from one another.

The heavy heel base
makes a slight click as

they press
together.

She stares at the double
union and asks

if he
likes them,

watching their dark
uniformed bolts

press into compliant
white leather.

Yes.
Yes.

Living in the Fog

You crept in under the door
like smoke dancing the limbo,
raising its arms to the sky.

I tried to keep you out,
not inhale you,
nor be caught by you,
fearing the moon would pull you from me
and the earth would stop turning.

Love entered anyway,
seeping through my pores.

I stand again at that same door
The moon has risen, set, and risen a lifetime now
Smoke has not cleared from my heart.
I live in that fog,
Loving you
Loving you even more.

Fallen Fruit

A man crosses the street carrying a pink bed pillow under his arm—
the too long pillow case trails in a breeze made of his rushing.

I watch from my car stopped at the crosswalk as he aims for the hospital
entrance—his stride purposeful, determined, his face etched with worry.

I'm overwhelmed with love for this stranger, for the simple gift of comfort
he brings from an empty bed at home. I should drive on, but sit wondering

if the pillow is for his wife, daughter, or maybe his mother. I think of my
own empty bed—think of all the different ways we can die.

The man steps from the crosswalk and passes beneath the shade of the monster
fig tree—a monument to constancy, this tree always dropping fruit, wasting

its sweetness on the unforgiving sidewalk. For a moment he is lost in the
    shadows,
a mere outline of a man, but I know him and how the wasted fruit feels
    underfoot—

the regret of it. I follow him until the familiar doors swallow him whole—
    the doors
I pass through daily leading to the hushed world of waterfalls, past the river
    of life

flowing through the courtyard where I gather calmness to take to my
    husband's
bedside, sit in vigilance armed with false cheer, as I rearrange his pillows
    from home.

My Man Buys in Bulk

                  and it makes me crazy
how he fills up the kitchen
like a squirrel   stores up hard for winter.
There's salt to last a lifetime   sugar
in brown paper sacks   a struggle to keep
from the ants.   Heaven forbid
          he should run out of granola.

I have given up weaning him
off this habit   just defend
            my breakfast station—
a tin of coffee beans
a flowered pitcher for cream   small
pottery jar of sugar.   And on the shelf above
a pint of honey   a four ounce
chocolate bar   a tasting jar of jam.

I have ceded the center cabinets   tall
and deep   clench my teeth when he enters
the kitchen door loaded down with supplies.
I kiss him and make myself scarce   until
           he's stored it all away.

Shopping for Godot

There are seventeen brands of water
on sale at Trader Joe's and I'm thinking
Smart Water
infused with lavender essence,

because I want to be smart,
and lavender sounds like a Spring meadow—
lovers and their children,
being chased by bees,
all the times I ran
and how good I got at running—
and I'm reaching for

grass-fed free-range
environmentally balanced beef
with an e-Coupon
redeemable for negative karma,

gluten free organic non-GMO Gala apples
each handcrafted by a wild
Arizona mustang's bastard Kachina-child.

It's such a relief to be healthy again.

My eyes stare hubble-blue at you.
I'm four inches taller than Jesus.
My abs are six-pack pop-top aphrodisiacs.

Oh dear love,
with eight reasons to doubt me,
put down your list and
help me carry these heavy bags.

Furious Bread

The yeast wakes up, faster than sourgrass after the rain.
I warm the old bowl on the pilot light, as my grandmother did,

scrape level the measure of flour using a knife's flat back.
There is no end to stubborn in this world. Even flour

fights like it would rather be grain again, recoils after every stretch,
the dough thick and heavy as a lump of potters' clay.

I push hard, throwing my weight behind each stroke,
arms stiff, lifting on my toes. Flatten, fold, turn, flatten, fold.

The newspaper on the table shows a senator. Resolved,
he says. One man, one woman. His God will not be swayed.

I pound the kneading board, knead until my wrists ache,
my skin crusted with salt, slowly will *yield*, will *suppleness*.

I round the dough to rest in the deep glazed bowl,
wait for rising, baking, food for those who sit at my table.

A Note of Thanks

"Honey, get it while you can."
—*Janis Joplin*

A well-kept black Buick crept through the parking lot
as if time no longer mattered, eventually found a spot
and cautiously, came to a stop.

Thank you elderly man in hip denim jacket and worn
baseball cap who creaked in slow motion around the back
to the passenger's side to aid a small woman,
her one daring toe touching pavement.

Thank you stylish high heel with striped sock,
frail and waiting

Thank you, practiced precision, their arms gently clutched,
easing her up

When steady, she held him with the wide smile of true love
while arranging a too-large sweater

Oh thank you, smile and tangled clothes

He leaned down low, eyes closed.
Even their kiss was slow.
Thank you.

V.

Poems by Children

Out Walking One Nice Day

Out walking one nice day
I saw a bush full of butterflies.
Butterfly bushes make me giggle!

All Yours

My wool blanket
with so many memories,
knitted by my late Gramma
is yours.
My books,
numbered in the thousands,
with just as many colors
is yours.
My lucky penny
given by a friend,
storing luck to use,
is yours.
My rainy day money,
saved for joy,
carefully stored,
is yours.
All that you need
can be yours
if you ask,
for a great man
named Ghandi
once said
"The fragrance
always remains in
the hand that
gives the rose."

Walking on Clouds

He sees me sitting up high in a tree. My dad
is watching me from up high in a cloud
and I am staring up at him.
When I stare up at him all I hear
are birds flying up high
and wind in my face. I can smell
the water from the river
but there's one thing
that I know is true, my dad,
holding my hand, and walking
right into the sunset with him.
Right there with me.

On a Beach Side Cliff

On a beach side cliff,
an unknown shape sparkled out loud;
It was a sunshine diamond!

My Voice

Stronger, stronger, voices can get.
Mad, exhausted, I run
to my room in a flurry.
I hide, my sister seeks.
She gets mad. I get mad.
She regrets it, I get sad.
She sticks a note under my door
and two minutes later
no one can even remember
what happened.

Gramma, Grandpa

Dear Gramma Carolyn,
I remember your hair, curly like spaghetti
strings. Your hair wanting to be as blond
as Marilyn Monroe but it has specks
of grey, like a pigeon sitting
on the roof of an old cottage.
I remember hearing the sports TV
as loud as can be because
Grandpa can't hear well.
I remember us in the plane
going to Utah, and me falling asleep
with my head on your lap.
Even though I snored like a pig
and tossed and turned, you didn't mind
because you loved me.

Dear Gramps,
I remember the bullet hole in your arm
from World War II.

I remember you dancing and singing
around the kitchen table. Even though
you are 90 nothing stops you
from getting a little hop in your step.

I remember your hair as white
as clouds on a summer day.

I remember me talking as loud
as a bird chirping to get your attention.

The Moon Can See Everything

When you are in bed...
she pokes out
through the soaking, wet
ocean water
streaming
down her body!
She sees
the whole bottom
of the ocean
at her feet tips,
she sees your loss in heaven.
She walks on the water
with a glowing bridge
for her to walk on!
Glowing,
her reflection glows!
She sees everything.

River

I want to be a river
as blue as the bluest lake
as fast as the strongest wind
yet I want to be swift
and fill all souls with delight
I want to be free
I want to be free

At dawn a hope to be calm
calm swift and sweet
In the blazing afternoon I will be rough
creating rapids at every turn
When dusk comes I shall be strong
strong and swift driving away fear
Oh how I want to change
I want to change

River River
Oh how I wish to be a river
River come to me change me
into the rushing river
that fills me with delight

Slam Poem

Competitive basketball makes me feel good.
Making baskets... Like a release of my anger.
I hear my teammates cheer me on.
Winning makes me proud.
Then I hear my annoying coach: "No, you're not doing it right!"
My body tenses. I get mad. I leave the game.
I take a break. I tell myself "You're doing it right."
I come back with a smile. *Play the game!*
Halfway through... I can't breathe. Running... I take six puffs from
my inhaler.
Coach says "You can stay out of the game!"
I tell him "No, Coach, I'm good."

Rather

(After "Rathers" by Mary Austin)

I know very well what I'd rather be
if I didn't always have to be me!
I'd rather be a Pomeranian,
a fluffy, soft Pomeranian,
a yippie-yappy, happy flappy
kind-eyed Pomeranian,
in a soft fluffy bed I'd bury my head,
I'd eat my dinner from a clean, shiny bowl,
running with my doggie friends,
if I were a yippie-yappy, happy flappy
kind-eyed Pomeranian,
And didn't always have to be me!

I know very well what I'd like to do
if I didn't have to do what I do!
I'd go and be a black panther
a sneaking, creeping, furry black panther
deep in the wet, flooded rainforest
on a hidden tree branch.
I'd never have to zoom in a single room,
ruling the rainforest splashing in the waters,
if I only had to do what I like to do
and didn't always have to be me.
Or I might be a parrot
A colorful parrot
A chatting, flapping parrot
Smart and ever watchful
I would sit to the side and take it all in.

But if I were an exotic animal vet
A smart caring vet—I'd like to be a vet—
I'd have a bag full of tools.
Happily I would come
to heal a sick, tired Pomeranian.
Wisely I would creep into rainforest to care
for the injured black panther.
I'd care for the scratchy tired voice
of the over talked parrot.
If he once met up with me.

Clouds Can Be Heaven

Remember when you were a river.
You are bored of being a river, then you see
water drops being sucked up. You close
your eyes, and when you finally open your eyes
you're no bad, dark, bloody, injured.
You're white, healthy, happy—
flying because of the wind.

After years, you become a big cloud.
You see angels everywhere,
you see my father sitting there,
watching me write this poem.

V.

POEMS IN SPANISH

Dios Sol

Mientras menos hablo
—más me empuja a caer
Sin pies
en los desfallecientes desfiladeros de los rayos del sol,
el silencio brilla por su ausencia—
Una voz resplandeciente aparece
en su espíritu, el horizonte magenta magnánimo.

Alabado el instante en que la lengua se alarga
y lame sus propias lágrimas
Lágrima expuesta
a una reflexión que se eleva de la boca del astro mayor.
Titubea en convertirse, allí, en un suspiro o aliento o vapor
—ahogado—despacio al comienzo
—intencionalmente—a dejarse ir
nada alcanza a gobernarla sin romperla.

Arriba—
con la cara hacia arriba, lejos
Precisamente cuando ya casi cae
pierde la sensación del viento solar en sus pulmones
de magma radiactivo perforados por el azar de una aguja desechada.

Mira su cara resguardando su corazón
que abre como una flor amazónica
con los sonidos de la exuberancia
¿los escuchas? ¿los escuchas agonizar en verde?

Mira a la tierra como un dios serpentino
que la abraza
Feliz
Feliz
Feliz

Efímera

Fuiste una burbuja en el aire
de colores arcoiris
rodeada de alegría
y muchos brazos extendidos para atraparte

Y tu,
caprichosa,
flotando sin dirección exacta
redonda,
prefecta,
luminosa,
transparente,
Etérea,
admirada,
Deseada.

Al mirarte
cómo te quise yo también
cómo te amé al tocarte
E f í m e r a

Caballitos de Totora

Tus melodías de coral me envuelven
pero tus espumas gaseosas no me tocan

Me envías mensajeras gaviotas
que de lado un solo ojo me vigilan
pero tampoco ellas me tocan.

Bajan gasas grises fantasmales de tu cielo
mientras tus olas saltan y se enojan.
Cierro por fin los ojos
y ella sale de tus aguas,
cuarto menguante su mirada
concha nácar sus colores,
peñas, brisas, sus olores
Eva marina, sí me toca,

Dos caballitos de totora en danza,
gallito y hembra de sangre hirviente
cuarto menguante cuarto creciente
arrastrados tormenta
en coro con las olas
gritan y repiten
amor, amor, amor.

A composition professor's tepid appraisal of **Ronald A. Alexander**'s early poetry interrupted Ron's writing for 25 years. Then in 1995, diagnosed yet surviving AIDS, he took a friend's advice: "If you're not going to die, write!" Together the two developed a novel of the AIDS pandemic. Yet, attending writer's conferences, Ron would steal away to poetry workshops. Eventually he could deny it no longer. He had succumbed to poetry.

Lisl Auf der Heide, born in Vienna, Austria, began writing poetry at age eight in her native German and continued writing, in English, after she emigrated to California at sixteen. Her work has appeared in various publications and anthologies as well as in seven collections of poetry. She has lived in Santa Barbara since 1970.

Rick Benjamin has published four books of poetry, most recently *Some Bodies in the Grief Bed* (forthcoming from Homebound Publications). His current project is a book about work that poetry helps us to do in our lives. He teaches at UCSB, Goleta Boys & Girls Club, Community Arts Workshop, a juvenile detention facility and elsewhere.

Daughter of a military family, **Ann Bennett** grew up in many places, and now calls Santa Barbara her home town, having lived here more than half of her life. She has written poetry off and on for most of her life, but rarely shared. She is delighted to be included here.

Gudrun Bortman grew up in Hamburg, Germany. She is an artist, garden designer and a poet. Her poems have been published in *Sukoon Literary Magazine*, *Panoply*, *San Pedro River Review*, *Miramar* and several anthologies published by Gunpowder Press. Her chapbook *Fireweed* was released in October 2018.

Jessica Bortman is an artist, writer, and business storytelling coach.

M. L. Brown is the author of *Call It Mist*, winner of the 2018 Three Mile Harbor Press Book Prize, and *Drought*, winner of the Claudia Emerson Chapbook award. Her work has appeared in *Valparaiso Poetry Review*, *Prairie Schooner*, and *Blackbird*, among other journals and anthologies.

Christopher Buckley has called Santa Barbara home since 1952. It has always been a source of inspiration. *Star Journal: Selected Poems*, *The Far Republics*, and *The Pre-Eternity of the World*, are recent books of poetry. His memoirs are *Cruising State*, *Sleep Walk*, and *Holy Days of Obligation*.

Molly Jane Burns has been writing poetry since early childhood. She received her B.A. in English with an Emphasis in Creative Writing from San Diego State University where her professors included Carolyn Forché and Glover Davis. A native Californian, her work has appeared in various local publications.

José María Carpizo went to a Jesuits high school in Mexico, where his Aesthetics teacher introduced him to the appreciation of the arts. In his class he read his favorite constellation of poets from the Spanish civil war era, "La Generación del 27." From there, Carpizo's love affair with poetry was born.

Eric M. Castro is a poet, a librarian, and an educator from Peru. He believes that poetry can change the world, and he uses it to inspire and empower young people in native communities of the Amazon rainforest in association with nonprofit organizations. Recently one of his poems was featured at the 2020 United Nations Day.

Susan Chiavelli is the recipient of the *Chattahoochee Review*'s Lamar York Nonfiction Prize for "Death, Another Country," also named a notable essay by *Best American Essays*. Her prose and poetry have appeared in *Paradise, Elsewhere, The Los Angeles Review, Miramar, San Pedro River Review, The Packinghouse Review*, and elsewhere.

Kundai Chikowero, a senior at Dos Pueblos High School, is an activist for social justice, community empowerment of underserved populations and anti-racism. She is a published poet who has won the Martin Luther King Jr. Essay and Poetry competition six times. Kundai was awarded the 2018 City of Santa Barbara Outstanding Youth Leader award.

Clayton Clark is a poet and painter who majored in Art History at UCLA. Born and raised in San Pedro, California, she now resides in Montecito. She's held many odd jobs, not the least of which involved raising two boys. Exploration and intense curiosity are the driving forces in her creative work.

Susan Read Cronin is best known for her playful bronze sculptures. She is the author of *Bronze Casting in a Nutshell* and in 2020 published *Notices*, her first chapbook of poetry. She is currently working on another book of poems. www.susanreadcronin.com

Frances Davis has written a column for *Coastal View News* for 25 years. Her work has appeared in the *L.A. Times, Passager, Calyx, The Chattahoochee Review, Askew, The Hopper from Green Writers Press*, and several Gunpowder Press anthologies. She is a winner of the Lamar York prize for nonfiction and also a Pushcart Prize nominee.

Pamela Davis's poems appear nationally and internationally in over 100 publications. Her first poetry book, *Lunette*, received the ABZ Poetry Prize in 2015. A native Californian, she is happiest hiking the local foothills and exploring France.

Margarita Delcheva is a poet, performer, and PhD candidate in Comparative Literature at UCSB. Margarita is a founding editor at Paperbag, an online poetry and art journal, created in 2009. Her poetry book *The Eight-Finger Concerto* was published in Bulgaria in 2010.

Andrea Ellickson writes novels about wildfire girls, Filipino legends, and family curses. She has traveled to over 30 countries to soak up stories and chase her curiosity. She currently works in the Department of Global Studies at UCSB, where she is eagerly waiting to travel again.

Joshua Escobar is the author of two chapbooks, *Caljforkya Voltage* and *xxox fm*, as well as a new debut collection, *Bareback Nightfall*, which explores a queer dystopia through the eyes of a deejay. He co-edits the student magazine *Open Fruit* at Santa Barbara City College.

Mary Freericks is the author of three volumes of poetry: *Blue Watermelon, Cheer for Freedom*, and *Furs for a Vegetarian*. She has an M.F.A. in poetry from Columbia University School of the Arts. Two poems, "Dream" and "The Bombing of Tabriz," were made into films by WildSound.

Maya Shaw Gale, MA, is a poet, spiritual guide and transformational life coach dedicated to midwifing clients from crisis and confusion to clarity and creative breakthrough. Her poetry has appeared in *Unmasked*, *The Pepper Lane Review I & II*, and her own book *The Last Wild Place*. She also facilitates women's writing and empowerment retreats.

Louise Borad Gerber started writing poetry to capture the emotional impact of life with her special needs daughter, resulting in her book *Naomi, My Baby Forever*. She continues writing poetry about the absurdities and realities of everyday life. Louise is also a part-time artist and has owned Closets, Etc. for 36 years.

Dr. Christina Gessler has written poetry since high school, attended college on a writing scholarship, and holds a Ph.D. in American history.

Cie Gumucio is a poet, artist and Poet/Teacher with Cal Poets in the Schools. Her solo exhibit *Writers in Search of the Sacred* explored the convergence of art, literature and spirituality. Cie has designed art installations with video, poetry, and dance and curated the TEDx event, Rediscovery of the Senses. She's won awards for writing in the film and television industry.

Ellen Hayward lives in Santa Barbara and has studied art and writing at SBCC Continuing Education, the Santa Barbara Writer's Conference, and the Santa Barbara Poetry Conference. Her work has been published in *Miramar*.

Born in Philadelphia to a family of campers and canoeists, **Roy Hildestad** pursued a career in engineering and math. After raising three wonderful sons in Santa Barbara, and retiring, his life-long fascination with meter and rhyme and his love of nature got together and took over an unused corner of his free time.

Linda L. Holland is a writer/musician. Her writing has been published in the *Cortland Review*, *Clean Run*, and the anthology *An Even Dozen*. Her music has won awards from ASCAP and has premiered at Carnegie and Wigmore Halls. Linda teaches at Santa Barbara City College.

Rebecca Horrigan is an English teacher and writer living in Santa Barbara. She enjoys writing for the *Santa Barbara Independent*, practicing yoga, listening to music, enjoying nature, and cooking.

Ibn Salma Ibrahim is a poet and a writer. He has a special connection to poetry, particularly poetry from the heart. He has made it his lifelong journey to discover the holiness within him as a spiritual being. His sources are sages from various traditions, lessons found within nature, and insights from his inner world.

e. j. has lived in Goleta all her life and has grown to be a passionate poetess, environmental and LGBTQ+ rights activist as well as an artistic entrepreneur with a driven mind that constantly thinks outside the box.

Eliot Jacobson is a retired professor of mathematics and computer science who has a lifelong love affair with poetry. He has published several poems over the years but considers himself to be more of an affectionate spectator than a writer himself.

Luci Janssen is a poet and lyricist. Her poems appear in the anthologies *Rare Feathers*, *Buzz*, and *To Give Life a Shape*. Luci 's poem "Beescape" appears in *Chasing Daphne*. Her poems are featured in the jazz album, *Artistry*. Luci's lyrics to "Once More" are published by A Muse Press.

Ellen Chavez Kelley teaches writing at UCSB and via California Poets in the Schools. Books include *Song for Highway 40* (Turning Point, 2012) and *In the Body of the Grove* (2008). Her picture book *My Life as a Chicken* (Harcourt, 2012) was a California Young Readers Award finalist.

Lois Klein has three poetry books: *Naming Water* (1998), *A Soldier's Daughter* (2008), and *Blooming Wild So Close to Home* (2013). She organizes the monthly Favorite Poems Project (currently through the Santa Barbara Public Library), teaches through the California Poets in the Schools Program, and leads private writing groups.

James Ph. Kotsybar is the first poet published to another planet. His poetry orbits Mars aboard NASA's MAVEN, appears in Hubble Space Telescope's mission log and was awarded at Centaur's 50th Anniversary

Art Challenge. Invited by EASAL's president, 2018, he performed before international scientists and Troubadours at EuroScience Open Forum.

Nancy Lee writes about childhood in a cramped apartment, Sunday sermons and Sunday suppers, cheap seats at Dodger Stadium, white go-go boots and her first copy of *Ms.* Magazine. Her poems appear in two volumes of *Pepper Lane Review*.

Shirley Geok-lin Lim's *Crossing the Peninsula* received the British Commonwealth Poetry Prize, first for a woman and Asian. She has 10 poetry collections, recently *The Irreversible Sun, Ars Poetica for the Day*, and *Do You Live In?* Her poems are: published in *Hudson Review, Feminist Studies, Virginia Quarterly Review*, and more; featured by Bill Moyers and on Tracey K. Smith's *Slowdown*; and performed in Poetry Out Loud.

Perie Longo, Santa Barbara Poet Laureate (2007-09), has published four books of poetry. She teaches poetry privately and is a psychotherapist and Registered Poetry Therapist who facilitates writing groups for wellness at Hospice and elsewhere believing that poetry inspires hope and healing, bridging the gap between self and others.

Jacqueline Lunianski has been reading and writing poetry for about 25 years. She enjoys shedding a light on everyday occurrences through her writing.

Teddy Macker is the author of the collection of poetry *This World*. He lives with his wife and daughters on a farm in Carpinteria, California, where he maintains an orchard.

Claudine Michel is Professor Emerita, Department of Black Studies, University of California. She is editor of the *Journal of Haitian Studies* and Executive Director of the Haitian Studies Association. Her poems appear in *Le Temps qui Passe* (Marlène Racine-Toussaint, editor), *Pawol Fanm sou Douz Janvye* (Gina Athena Ulysse, guest editor), a special issue of *Meridians. Feminism. Race. Transnationalism*, and elsewhere.

Kathee Miller, a professor of depth psychology, has been writing as long as she can remember, from her origins in New York to California, bringing a deep embodied connection to music, art, memory and place.

Various books—*Pepper Lane Review, Rare Feathers, To Give Life a Shape, Women's Mysteries*—and journals contain her poetry.

Anne Neubauer is a writer and poet and has a deep love of literature. Her poetry is inspired by daily time spent in the quiet of the natural world near the Pacific Ocean in both northern and southern California.

Enid Osborn served as Poet Laureate of Santa Barbara from 2017 to 2019. The poems in *When The Big Wind Comes* (2015) take place during her childhood in Southeast New Mexico. She co-edited *A Bird Black as the Sun: California Poets on Crows & Ravens*, and has completed seven chapbooks and a new manuscript, *Little Wakes*.

Since immigrating from Ireland, **Dairine Pearson** has lived in Goleta for over 30 years. She works as a grief counselor and finds solace and healing in nature, music, movement and poetry.

Christine Penko is the author of *Thunderbirds*, a memoir in poetry, published in 2015. Her work can also be found in journals and anthologies under the name Christine Kravetz. Recent publications include *Prairie Schooner* and *Miramar*. She taught poetry in Santa Barbara schools, and was the area administrator for California Poets.

Peg Quinn has a B.F.A. in Education from the University of Nebraska and is a visual artist and educator. Her poetry and creative non-fiction have been published in numerous journals and anthologies and three-times nominated for the Pushcart Prize. Her debut book, *Mother Lode*, was published by Gunpowder Press in 2021.

Diana Raab, MFA, Ph.D., is a poet, memoirist, blogger, and award-winning author of ten books. Her latest books are *Writing for Bliss* and *Lust: Poems*. She blogs for *Psychology Today, The Wisdom Daily, Thrive Global*, and others. She frequently speaks and facilitates workshops on writing for healing and transformation.

Tamara Zdenek Riley is a commercial/residential interior designer and owner of Tamara Riley Design. When she is not designing homes, cooking, or playing tennis, you'll find her on a spiritual journey traveling the globe writing about her experiences.

Sojourner Kincaid Rolle is a poet, playwright, environmental educator and peace activist. She served as Santa Barbara's Poet Laureate from 2015-2017. Her books include *Mellow Yellow Global Umbrella*, *Common Ancestry*, and *Black Street: Poems*. Rolle has led workshops through her Song of Place Poetry Project since 1997.

Shelly Rosen is an actor and a poet. He has acted for fifty-seven years, recently as Doc in an original play, *XOXO God*. He also wrote and performed in a one-man showcase. Finding great joy in writing, Shelly works on poems every day. Poetry is his constant companion.

Nicolasa I. Sandoval, Ph.D. (Santa Ynez Band of Chumash Indians) is an educator, musician, and writer. She resides in Lompoc with her husband, John Gustafsson, and their beloved canine companions, Boman and Georgia.

Greg Spencer has taught communication studies at Westmont for over thirty years. He has written five books, including *Awakening the Quieter Virtues* and *Reframing the Soul*. Next up is a semi-autobiographical novel called *Boomer Boy*. He loves being married. He and Janet have six grandchildren, all of whom know that the secret word is binka-bonka.

David Starkey served as Santa Barbara's 2009-2011 Poet Laureate and is Director of the Creative Writing Program at Santa Barbara City College. He is Co-editor and Publisher of Gunpowder Press, as well as the author of eight full-length poetry collections.

Daniel Thomas's collection of poetry, *Deep Pockets*, won a 2018 Catholic Press Award. He has published poems in many journals, including *Southern Poetry Review*, *Nimrod*, *Poetry Ireland Review*, *Atlanta Review*, and others. He has an MFA in poetry from Seattle Pacific University, as well as an MA in film and a BA in literature.

Emma Trelles is the author of *Tropicalia*, winner of the Andrés Montoya Poetry Prize. She is currently writing a second book of poems, *Courage and the Clock*, and has received writing fellowships from CantoMundo and the Florida Division of Cultural Affairs. She teaches at Santa Barbara City College and curates the Mission Poetry Series.

When not writing poems, **Jace Turner** is most likely taking long walks, reading, visiting friends, or making a mess in the kitchen.

Sydney Vogel is a teenager from Santa Ynez. She enjoys knitting, reading or watching sci-fi, tabletop gaming with friends, and learning as much about the world as she possibly can.

Isabelle Walker is a Santa Barbara-based poet and teacher with a special interest in the natural world and recovery. Her poem about the January 2018 Montecito debris flow won first prize in Seven Hills Review's 2018 Literary & Penumbra Poetry Contest. She has an MFA in Creative Writing from Antioch University Los Angeles.

Mark Walker grew up on military bases around the word, settling in Austin Texas from 1973-2001. After moving to Santa Barbara in 2001, Mark started songwriting at City College Continuing Education (taught by Nicola Gordon). He and his wife, Jan Ziegler, run 10 West Gallery.

Carol Ann Wilburn has been writing poetry since childhood but only recently began compiling her first chapbook. To jumpstart her dream to be a published writer, she submitted poems to *While You Wait*. After a long career in theatre management, she served on the boards of the Granada Theatre and Ensemble Theatre Company, affirming her belief in the power of the arts to inspire people's lives.

Bruce Willard has published two collections of poems, *Holding Ground* (2013) and *Violent Blues* (2016), both published by Four Way Books. His third collection, *In Light of Stars*, is expected in 2021.

Paul Willis has published six collections of poetry, the most recent of which is *Little Rhymes for Lowly Plants* (White Violet Press). His latest book is a YA Elizabethan time-travel novel, *All in a Garden Green* (Slant). He is a professor of English at Westmont College and a former poet laureate of Santa Barbara.

Ann Michener Winter is a CA native and has been writing poetry, prose and creative non-fiction since age 11. She enjoys reading, gardening, travel and family and friends.

George Yatchisin is the author of *Feast Days* (Flutter Press 2016) and *The First Night We Thought the World Would End* (Brandenburg Press 2019). He is co-editor of *Rare Feathers: Poems on Birds & Art* (Gunpowder Press 2015), and his poetry appears in anthologies including *Reel Verse: Poems About the Movies* (Everyman's Library 2019).

Estella Ye recently discovered a new mantra, namely "All Izz Well" from the movie "3 Idiots." It resonates with her as a somewhat stressed first-time student at SBCC. For years, she learned poetry at the Santa Barbara Music and Arts Conservatory, under the guidance of Chryss Yost and George Yatchisin and studied classical piano and violin.

Chryss Yost, Ph.D., is a Santa Barbara Poet Laureate (2013-15) and co-editor of Gunpowder Press. Her poems have been widely published in anthologies and journals, most recently in *SALT*. As a heart attack survivor, she raises awareness about Spontaneous Coronary Artery Dissection (SCAD) and heart health.

Marilee Zdenek is the author of seven books, including *The Right-Brain Experience* which has been published in six languages. She has taught at the Santa Barbara Writers Conference since the 1980's and served on the Board of Directors at Hospice of Santa Barbara for nine years.

Photo by Stacey J. Byers

ABOUT THE EDITOR

Laure-Anne Bosselaar, Santa Barbara Poet Laureate (2019-2021), is the author of *The Hour Between Dog and Wolf*, *Small Gods of Grief* (winner of the Isabella Gardner Prize for Poetry), and *A New Hunger* (an ALA Notable Book). The editor of four previous anthologies, her poems have been featured on The Academy of American Poets' *Poem-a-Day*, *Poetry Daily*, and *The Writer's Almanac*. Her poems have been published in journals including *Orion*, *Georgia Review*, *Ploughshares*, and *Five Points*. She won the 2021 James Dickey Prize and is the recipient of a Pushcart Prize. She taught at Sarah Lawrence College, and teaches at the Solstice Low Residency MFA Program. Her latest collection of poems, *These Many Rooms*, was published by Four Way Books in 2019.

BARRY SPACKS POETRY PRIZE SERIES

2015
Instead of Sadness
Catherine Abbey Hodges

2016
Burning Down Disneyland
Kurt Olsson

2017
Posthumous Noon
Aaron Baker

2018
The Ghosts of Lost Animals
Michelle Bonczek Evory

2019
Drinking with O'Hara
Glenn Freeman

2020
Curriculum
Meghan Dunn

Also from Gunpowder Press

The Tarnation of Faust: Poems by David Case

Mouth & Fruit: Poems by Chryss Yost

Shaping Water: Poems by Barry Spacks

Original Face: Poems by Jim Peterson

What Breathes Us: Santa Barbara Poets Laureate, 2005-2015
Edited by David Starkey

Unfinished City: Poems by Nan Cohen

Raft of Days: Poems by Catherine Abbey Hodges

Mother Lode: Poems by Peg Quinn

and the Shoreline Voices Projects:

Buzz: Poets Respond to SWARM
Edited by Nancy Gifford and Chryss Yost

Rare Feathers: Poems on Birds & Art
Edited by Nancy Gifford, Chryss Yost, and George Yatchisin

To Give Life a Shape: Poems Inspired by the Santa Barbara Museum of Art
Edited by David Starkey and Chryss Yost

CPSIA information can be obtained
at www.ICGtesting.com
Printed in the USA
BVHW030550050521
606419BV00005B/912